Educating for Christian Maturity

Neil Parent
General Editor

Department of Education
United States Catholic Conference

In its 1990 planning document, as approved by the general membership of the United States Catholic Conference in November 1989, the Department of Education was authorized to continue with the publication of an annual resource book for adult religious education. This current publication, *Educating for Christian Maturity,* was prepared by Mr. Neil A. Parent, Coordinator of the Division of Catechesis/Religious Education, approved by Sr. Lourdes Sheehan, RSM, Secretary of Education, and authorized for publication by the undersigned.

Monsignor Robert N. Lynch
General Secretary
NCCB/USCC

First printing, June 1990
Second printing, October 1997

ISBN 1-55586-347-7

Contents

Introduction / 1
Neil Parent

I. The Challenge of Christian Maturity / 5
James J. Bacik

Meaning and Maturity: Adult Education's Response / 14
Mary Jo Klase

II. A Contemporary Spirituality for Mature Christians / 21
Robert F. Morneau

Participating in the Holy
Challenges for a Twenty-First Century Church / 32
Jack McBride

III. Clothed in Strength and Seasoned, She Flourishes / 39
Ann Johnson

Rummaging through Maturity / 49
Alice Stefaniak

IV. What Prevents Adult Christians from Becoming Mature? / 53
Dennis L. O'Connor

Aiding the Conversion Process
A Challenge for Adult Educators / 64
Edmund F. Gordon

V. Christian Maturation: The Later Years / 71
Janice Brewi, CSJ, and Anne Brennan, CSJ

Helping Mid-Lifers in Their Spiritual Journey / 82
Loretta Girzaitis

About the Authors / 87

Introduction

Human maturity has an elusive quality to it. By definition, *maturity* means full development. But there are so many aspects to human development—physical, intellectual, emotional, social, spiritual—that its attainment across the spectrum is clearly beyond our reach. Indeed, with the possible exception of the physical, even a single dimension of maturity will ultimately elude us. We can always aspire to greater maturity; we can always entertain the possibility of more personal integration, more wisdom, more love of God. Maturity is a goal that has no defined end point.

Much has been written about the interrelationship among the various aspects of maturity. Spiritual maturity, for example, is not one-dimensional. It is not simply a matter of addressing the spiritual side of our personality, as if that could somehow be isolated within us. Rather, authentic spiritual maturity depends upon a holistic integration of the mind and the body, the heart and the will, the personal and the relational. All aspects of the human person have their role to play in spiritual growth. All of them need to coalesce fruitfully in our ongoing quest for God.

The Scriptures present Jesus as a paradigm of spiritual maturity, both in terms of what he accomplished and how he accomplished it. Jesus achieved a spiritual maturity so pronounced that those who met him could say—at least with graced hindsight—that he was the living embodiment of God.

Luke tells us that Jesus "advanced [in] wisdom and age and favor before God and man" (Lk 2:52). Jesus did not arrive at spiritual maturity as if by gift but, rather, as the result of his steadfast and courageous response to what he perceived as his Father's will. He prayed often and long. He fasted and observed other requirements of the *Torah*. He heeded the needs of the poor and suffering. He offered up his own life in witness and service.

Following the path of Jesus has been the primary vocation of Christians down through the ages. Their desire has been to become like him, to become with him and in him, spiritually mature. Indeed, St. Paul exhorts Christians to "attain to the unity of faith and knowledge of the Son of God . . . so that we may no longer be infants . . ." (Eph 4:13).

Each age and culture must apply the model of Jesus to its own times and circumstances. The question of what constitutes Christian maturity must be answered afresh by each generation. What first-century Christians in Antioch thought about being Christlike would be vastly different from those in pre-Reformation Europe or from those of us in the United States at the close of the twentieth century. Christians of every era and location seek to model Christ out of their own experiences of the world, with their different needs and responsibilities, with their vastly different self-concepts. As Carl Jung once noted, "The person whose sun still moves around the earth is essentially different from the person whose earth is a satellite of the sun."

While there is much of Christian maturity that is common down through the ages and across cultures, the differences are more than accidental. They belong to the essence of how Christian maturity is incarnated at a particular moment in history.

It was for this reason that the National Advisory Committee on Adult Religious Education (NACARE) set about a few years ago to address the topic of "contemporary Christian maturity." As NACARE saw it, unless there was a sufficient understanding of what constitutes contemporary Christian maturity, adult educators would lack clear direction in their efforts. After all, the goal of adult religious education, as with all catechesis, is to foster mature faith in learners (cf. *Sharing the Light of Faith: National Catechetical Directory for Catholics of the United States* [= NCD], 33).

This collection of articles, then, was commissioned by NACARE with the hope that it would serve adult educators to help learners grow more deeply, more maturely in their faith.

Educating for Christian Maturity consists of ten articles focusing on five broad issues: (1) dimensions of Christian maturity; (2) a spirituality for mature Christian faith; (3) a feminine perspective on Christian maturity; (4) hindrances to Christian maturity; and (5) Christian maturity in the later years. Each issue is addressed twice: first, from a theoretical perspective and then with an emphasis on practical application.

Drawing upon the Christian anthropology of Karl Rahner, James Bacik explores five dialectics of Christian maturity. Mary Jo Klase uses Leon McKenzie's paradigm of lifelong learning to draw adult education implications from Bacik's article.

Bishop Robert Morneau of Green Bay uses a rich mixture of prose and poetry to describe a contemporary spirituality for mature Christians. Jack McBride builds on Morneau's theme of the holy to identify several challenges facing the Church in general, and educators in particular.

Rich with biblical sources and images, Ann Johnson presents an evocative perspective of feminine spiritual maturity. Alice Stefaniak offers some reflection exercises to enable readers to image their own maturity.

Dennis O'Connor explores the obstacles to Christian maturity, particularly through the twin lenses of self-knowledge and conversion. Building on O'Connor's themes, Edmund Gordan identifies several challenges facing adult educators who seek to work with learners using a conversion model.

Finally, Janice Brewi and Anne Brennan tap Jungian psychology and spiritual tradition to describe the unique opportunities awaiting Christians in the second half of life. Loretta Girzaitis offers several recommendations to adult educators for dealing with the issues raised by Brewi and Brennan.

What became abundantly clear to me in putting this book together is the vast complexity and richness of the topic of "Christian maturity." There is so much more that we as a Church can and should say about it.

Each one of us who struggles with the daily call of our Christian vocation has some valuable insight into what comprises Christian maturity. Our challenge as a Church today is to figure out how we might bring together these individual insights so that we can all benefit from having a more complete picture. To whatever extent we can do this, we will all be the richer.

Neil A. Parent
General Editor
Division of Catechesis/Religious Education
Department of Education
United States Catholic Conference

The Challenge of Christian Maturity

James J. Bacik

Sarah, a middle-aged Catholic, had returned to college to study psychology. She had grown up in a rather repressive Catholic family, ingesting in the process large amounts of neurotic guilt. As a youngster, she had been taught that nice girls are submissive and dependent. At the age of twenty, she quit school and entered into a traditional marriage in which her husband was clearly the dominant partner. Now, after twenty-five years of a rather unsatisfying marriage, her studies were opening up an exciting new world for her. She was learning about self-actualization and developing her potential. The messages given in her class were that she could be anyone that she wanted to be. It seemed to her that some of the younger women in her class had a very different outlook on themselves and their relationships to men. They seemed to be stronger and more independent than she ever remembered being.

Somehow, all this new learning was calling into question Sarah's traditional Catholic faith. Her religion now appeared as an obstacle to her self-growth. It seemed as though she would have to jetison her faith if she were ever to reach the kind of maturity for which she now longed. The guilt feelings would have to go if she was ever to feel good about herself and tap her potential. She would have to rid herself of a religion that called upon her to be passive and dependent.

Sarah ended up in my office because she worried that in giving up her Catholic religion she might be losing something that was truly important to her. Part of my task was to help her discover the positive resources in her religious heritage that could assist her in the process of self-growth.

Sarah, who likes to share the story of her continuing appropriation of those Christian resources, represents for me some of the crucial challenges as well as the opportunities facing many who are striving for greater Christian maturity. Her story raises the fundamental question of whether the two terms *Christian* and *maturity* can comfortably fit together, or whether they are in some sort of essential contradiction, as many influential thinkers of the nineteenth and twentieth centuries have contended. Karl Marx, for instance, made the well-known claim that religion functions as an opiate, which prevents believers from assuming their proper responsibilities for creating a better world. Friedrich Nietzsche insisted that Christian belief keeps people from creating their own values. According to him, individuals who take the excessively meek Jesus of Nazareth as their model will never be able to take hold of their own lives and become mature and powerful individuals. Sigmund Freud contended that theism is a projection and an obsessive neurosis that keeps persons in an infantile state. Jean-Paul Sartre taught that belief in an omnipotent God destroys human freedom, thereby making full maturation impossible.

These influential critics of religion have helped create a general impression that Christianity is essentially dehumanizing and inevitably keeps people from developing their potential and becoming more mature. For these great critics and their followers, the terms *Christian* and *maturity* are indeed antithetical.

In *The Humanist Manifesto II,* published in 1973, we find an updated version of the charge that religion is fundamentally a detriment to human growth. This document, which sets out seventeen principles for creating a better secular society, makes the assumption that genuine humanists must be *nontheists.* In their very first thesis, the authors claim that religion creates dependencies and escapisms, "impeding the free use of the intellect." They insist that promises of immortal salvation or fear of eternal damnation are harmful, distracting human beings from the whole process of self-actualization. The document goes on to say that orthodox religions inculcate repressive attitudes toward sexuality, thereby preventing people from developing a mature and responsible attitude toward that vital aspect of their lives. After stating their seventeen major principles, the authors declare in their conclusion: "We urge that parochial loyalties and inflexible moral and religious ideologies be transcended." Although the authors admit in one place that "religion may inspire dedication to the highest ethical ideals," the whole tenor of their manifesto is that religion impedes human growth and keeps individuals from becoming mature persons.

Sarah's story also suggests the negative effects of our patriarchal society on the process of maturation. Influenced by a patriarchal ideology, we tend to define maturity in terms of stereotypical male qualities. Thus, the mature person thinks logically and rationally, is cool under pressure, and is not afraid to use power to control and dominate. The well-known stages of moral development, proposed by Lawrence Kohlberg, suggest that the most mature people make moral judgments according to general, abstract principles. It is interesting to note that he did his initial studies with men only, and that men generally rate higher than women on his scale of moral development.

As feminist theologian, Rosemary Ruether, points out, destructive dualistic thinking is at the heart of the patriarchal ideology. According to this dualistic thinking, sharp dichotomies exist between spirit and matter, soul and body, male and female, human and nonhuman, grace and nature. In patriarchal societies, which reflect this thinking, males are considered superior to women because they are fully mature individuals endowed with the power of reason. On the other hand, women are considered to be inferior because they are identified with matter, body, and nature. Patriarchal societies naturally hand over to males the power to determine the very definition of maturity. In the process, important human qualities are left out. Given this situation, it is impossible to speak effectively about Christian maturity without attacking patriarchy and the dualisms that undergird it.

Many critics contend that the Judeo-Christian tradition has fostered this kind of patriarchal society. The normative Scriptures were written by men who considered women to be inferior and used God to justify the existing patterns of domination. By its sexist practices, the Church continues to promote the myth of male superiority. When women's experience is systematically denied or erased, it is difficult for the Church to proclaim a credible ideal of the mature life.

In summary, all of the forces of dehumanization in the modern world present themselves as a challenge to the struggle for Christian maturity. As a first step in meeting this challenge, we Christians need a credible ideal of maturity that can overcome all the charges that religion is essentially dehumanizing and that Christianity is in evitably sexist.

A Christian Response

In working out a contemporary understanding of Christian maturity, we can begin by examining our own experience. We sense deep within ourselves a call to develop the gifts that we have received. Despite our failures, we know the drive to become our better selves. Our minds and our hearts search for truth and for goodness. The disappointments and failures of life threaten to drag us down, but they can also function as a stimulus for further growth. Our best moments come when we respond wholeheartedly to the call to move toward greater balance, integration, responsibility, and interdependence, guided in the process by love and care. The dream of such maturity has a surprising power to challenge our complacency and to draw us out of our selfishness and isolation.

Our Christian tradition helps us to illumine this call to growth. We believe in a God who is the source of our dynamism and the goal of all of our striving. Our Scriptures tell us that it is the divine spirit that calls us to put aside childish ways and to live with greater maturity (cf. 1 Cor 14:20). For Christians, Jesus Christ remains the model of the mature person. By encountering Christ, we sense the depth and extent of our own potential, as well as the divine call to become our better selves. By living as true disciples, we can grow to full maturity in Christ (cf. Eph 4:15).

Through his death and resurrection, Christ poured out his Spirit upon all of us, energizing and guiding us to develop our potential. The Spirit of Christ enables us to recognize and transform the dehumanizing tendencies in our culture that block the path to greater maturity.

The same Spirit binds all human beings together in a unity that is deeper than all the divisions based on gender, race, and status (cf. Gal 3:28). The divine Spirit, who inhabits the entire universe and guides the whole evolutionary process, undercuts all the dualisms that plague our patriarchal culture.

Furthermore, the Scriptures remind us that the development of our potential has a larger purpose: "To each individual the manifestation of the Spirit is given for some benefit" (1 Cor 12:7). Channeling our energies toward the service of others enables us to be more receptive to the Spirit, who can accomplish surprising things in us (cf. Jn 3:8).

The Scriptures thus remind us that the drive toward maturity is really a call from God. The life of Christian maturity is not a vague idea, but rather a clear and compelling ideal, revealed in the New Testament witness to Jesus Christ. We move toward this ideal, not in isolation, but guided by the Holy Spirit. Maturity is not an individual achievement, but must be placed in the service of others.

The Second Vatican Council has helped to specify this biblical teaching. Following the direction of the council's *Pastoral Constitution on the Church in the Modern World*, we can see that the call to Christian maturity is rooted in the dignity of human persons. Every individual is a "living image of God" and possesses a "godlike seed."

This intimate relationship with God does not reduce our freedom, but rather liberates us to pursue our fulfillment and happiness with greater meaning. Since we live in a community of persons made in the image of God, any maturity that we have attained carries with it responsibilities to care for the other members of the community. The drive for Christian maturity is not a self-contained autonomous effort to achieve self-fulfillment. On the contrary, it is a Spirit-inspired call to a life of service that should always remain open to the divine.

This brief glance at highlights of the Christian tradition suggests that one good way of responding to the charge that religion is dehumanizing is by a positive effort to articulate and celebrate the ideal of Christian humanism. We must not let the atheistic and secular humanists co-opt the ideals and the language of the best of the humanistic tradition.

The terms *Christianity* and *humanism* are not antithetical. On the contrary, at the deepest level, they are mutually inclusive.

Christianity calls individuals to full human development, and a genuine humanism is open to the transcendent Source proclaimed by Jesus. Christian humanism fruitfully combines the positive meanings and values in the culture with the guiding and inspiring light of faith.

It recognizes the power of reason and the accomplishments of science, while insisting that intelligence is broader than reason and that Christianity possesses a better worldview than science. It celebrates the cultural ideal of self-actualization and, at the same time, reminds us that personal development should bring us closer to God.

Christian humanism calls us to participate in political life as a way of spreading the kingdom of justice and love. It leads us to a deep appreciation of human culture, which enables us to discern the signals of transcendence in all authentic forms of cultural life. Moreover, Christian humanists recognize that the maturation process is never totally completed. They believe in the power of the Holy Spirit to bring new life and surprising transformations. For believers, the quest for maturity is a lifelong adventure, which is fulfilled only when we are finally united with the Lord.

The Christian faith has produced a long history of humanistic development, as well as great people who have lived out humanistic values. Our analysis suggests that the positive ideals of maturity espoused by *The Humanist Manifesto* can be best achieved within the framework of faith in Christ.

The broad outlines of maturity suggested by Christian humanism need greater specification in order to gain a hearing in the contemporary world. The great theologians of our time can help us in this task. I find special enlightenment and inspiration in the work of the German Jesuit, Karl Rahner (1904-1984).

Rahner developed a theological anthropology or an understanding of human existence that provides a solid foundation for understanding and achieving Christian maturity. For him, all human beings are oriented to the infinite. We are all called to surrender ourselves to the incomprehensible mystery in rule over our lives. We are a mysterious combination of infinite longings and finite capabilities. Our dignity is found in our ability to hear and to answer the call of the great God.

According to Rahner's anthropology, we move toward greater maturity by achieving a fruitful synthesis between apparently opposing tendencies competing within our minds and hearts. This principle can be clarified by simply indicating some of the dialectical relationships found in Rahner's extensive and penetrating analysis of human existence.

We are self-transcendent creatures with untapped potential, who can achieve maturity only by accepting our limitations and submitting ourselves to the Mystery we call God. We are unique individuals responsible for ourselves, who can find fulfillment only by living out our social nature in various personal communities. We are spiritual creatures with an unlimited horizon, who, at the same time, must live as physical, sexual, and historical human beings, immersed in the world of time and space. We are personal subjects called to be a unified whole, who are threatened by the estrangement of sin and guilt that block our path to maturity. We are infinite questioners called to an intelligent pursuit of personal development, who can achieve genuine knowledge and authentic maturity only by becoming better lovers. We have the ability to shape our future but only under the influence of our past history. Finally, we gain maturity by reaching out to others, but we can be effective in our outreach only by developing a rich interior life.

From the perspective of Rahnerian anthropology, the mature individual appears as an exciting energetic synthesis of apparently opposed forces existing in a fruitful tension. The human person is, as Rahner contends, "spirit in the world," a mysterious combination of infinite longings and finite capabilities. We move toward maturity by being deeply rooted in the real world and, at the same time, being open to the call of the infinite echoing in the finite. Mature people understand that they are oriented to the Gracious Mystery—the One who calls us to put on the mind of Christ and to become more and more responsive to the Spirit.

Rahner's anthropology suggests that the journey to Christian maturity requires the development of dialectical virtues. Virtues are assured capacities that enable us to respond effectively to very diverse situations. They are like a second nature that enables us to move toward maturity in a spontaneous and open fashion, without the fatigue generated by fighting ourselves. Virtues that have a dialectical character combine opposing tendencies in a synthesis that is vivifying and energizing. They represent a middle way between extreme tendencies characterized by immaturity.

From another perspective, we can think of these paired opposites as marks of maturity or ideals that can encourage and guide individuals in their efforts to achieve genuine adulthood. If we want to make the journey to Christian maturity, it is helpful to have not only a grand vision, but also a more detailed map. The following descriptions of five dialectical virtues are designed to provide some of that detail.

1. Committed Openness

Mature individuals are able to guard against both a mindless relativism that judges one position to be as good as another, and a narrow exclusivism that tries to monopolize truth and goodness. They achieve instead a free and intelligent commitment to their particular standpoint, which in turn enables them to pass over with confidence to the standpoints of others, in search for meaning and value greater than they currently possess. In order to move in this direction, we should strive, for example, to root ourselves so firmly in our religious tradition that we possess the confidence to be open to truth and goodness wherever they are found. A commitment to our religious heritage, which is based on a genuine understanding and appreciation of both its strengths and weaknesses, is precisely what will enable us to enter into a fruitful dialogue with other traditions. Christian maturity involves dedication to Christ, which leads to a healthy openness in all aspects of life.

2. *Reflective Spontaneity*

In our culture, we are in danger of falling into either an excessive and paralyzing introspection or a superficial, unexamined immersion in the activities of life. Mature individuals are able to combine a spontaneous involvement in the present moment with periodic self-examination, which in turn frees them to live more fully in the now.

Most of us see this as an attractive virtue. We want to live in a self-forgetful way, but this requires self-examination. It is desirable to be attentive to our current experience, but this seems to be facilitated by regular meditation. Our goal is to participate wholeheartedly in the events of our lives, but we need insight and understanding to do so. This means that we must find a proper frequency and method for our reflective times so that they do not increase our anxiety and preoccupation with self, but rather help free us to listen to the God who speaks to us in the present moment. Individuals who have put on the mind of Christ seek out their quiet times with the Lord so they can follow his will in the midst of the busyness of life.

3. *Hopeful Realism*

Contemporary culture tempts us to swing from a naive optimism to a cynical pessimism as ideals are tarnished and dreams unfulfilled. In reaction, we must strive for a spiritual maturity that is in touch with reality, including its dark and tragic dimension, but which maintains a lively confidence in the ultimate triumph of good over evil. At the same time, we must be aware of the signals of hope in our everyday experience that remind us of God's final victory over suffering. Christian maturity will be credible today only if it appears to be realistic and, at the same time, offers hope in the face of complex problems.

4. *Enlightened Simplicity*

Some people find themselves fixated in a childish religious outlook that ignores the ambiguity of life and runs on emotion divorced from reason. Others are trapped in a pseudo-sophistication in which a little bit of knowledge has obscured the whole point of authentic religion. Mature persons avoid these tendencies in a variety of ways: by striving for a spirituality that includes a purity of heart founded on an adequate theology; by practicing a humble charity based on insight; by living out an uncomplicated life-style, intelligently chosen and directed; and by cultivating a total dependence on God, matched by a creative use of their talents.

To move in this direction, we need an adult understanding of our faith, one that recognizes the simple good news that there is a gracious God, who loves us despite our unworthiness. Mature Christians are not immune from doubts, but they have a simple confidence that the Spirit is guiding them toward a deeper understanding of themselves and their world.

5. Prayerfully Prophetic

It is not uncommon today to find people very serious about prayer, but lacking concern for the needs of the oppressed and disadvantaged. On the other hand, some people who are serious about improving our world find prayer irrelevant to that task. To avoid such one-sidedness, mature believers develop a prayer life that intensifies their awareness of social injustice and moves them to prophetic action on behalf of those enslaved by oppressive systems. At the same time, involvement in the struggle to humanize the world sends them back to prayer, where they recall their dependence upon God and seek new energy and strength for the struggle. Christian maturity today calls for a liberation spirituality that taps the power of the Spirit in all of the work for justice and peace.

As this brief analysis suggests, Rahner's theological anthropology gives us a dialectical sense of Christian maturity. His analysis strikes many of us as faithful to our own experience of struggling to keep opposed tendencies in some sort of proper balance. We know this battle deep within ourselves. Our sense is that we are moving in the right direction when we refuse to collapse either side of the dialectic, but find ways of achieving integration within this struggle.

In order to achieve this integration, we must be attentive to all the dimensions of our existence, including the physical, emotional, imaginative, intellectual, moral, and religious facets of our complex personalities. Ideally, mature Christians respect their bodies, making them better symbols of their spirit through proper exercise, diet, and sleep. They tap their complex affective life, recognizing and mobilizing all their emotions for personal growth and service to the community. Their imaginations are stirred by Jesus Christ and shaped by the gospel. They use their intelligence to seek the wisdom of God, revealed in Christ—a wisdom that integrates all knowledge through the power of love, reveals the secrets of the human heart, and confounds the wisdom of the world. Their moral life is characterized by a generous response to the call of God, leading to the pursuit of goodness and virtue even when these higher goods conflict with desire and satisfaction. Finally, mature Christians have fallen in love with God, entrusting themselves to the Gracious Mystery revealed in Jesus Christ, who loves them without restriction or condition.

Since this kind of religious maturity engenders trust and commitment, it facilitates growth in all the other dimensions of human existence. If we believe God is on our side and accepts us as we are, then we are free to face our limitations and, with the Lord's help, to rise above our failures. In this way, we do indeed gradually move toward greater maturity as the sons and daughters of God.

Conclusion

As the story of Sarah suggests, the challenges to Christian maturity are intensified in the modern world. In order to counter the charge of dehumanization, we must proclaim and live out a credible and attractive Christian humanism. To transform the contradictions built into a patriarchal society, we must strive for a Christian maturity that is rooted in the power of the Spirit to reconcile all divisions and overcome all dualisms.

Our discussion of maturity from the viewpoint of the Scriptures and contemporary theology offers others some guidance in pursuing this ideal of Christian maturity. It is also an invitation to find our own way and to tap other resources in our rich heritage.

In this effort, it is important to remember that Christian maturity is a goal toward which we move—without ever arriving. As Karl Rahner suggested, we are Christians in order to become better Christians. We must learn to accept this reality and to live easily with this tension, confident that the Gracious Mystery sustains and guides our journey to greater maturity in Christ.

Meaning and Maturity
Adult Education's Response

Mary Jo Klase

Shortly after my husband's death, I was assigned the task of reading *Seasons of Strength*[1] for a course I was taking. The authors' focus was on our journey with God toward maturity. The guiding themes were *vocation* and *virtue*, two images central to Christian spirituality. The major dynamic was *imagination*.

The authors invited the reader to envision life as a vocation, as a movement from child of God in the early years, to disciple of the Lord in the young adult years, to steward of the faith in the mature years. They imaged virtues as a constellation of powers functioning in partnership within the person, their energies fueling the movement of maturation. In *Seasons of Strength*, I discovered a model for both professional reflection and personal re-creation.

In the foregoing article, "The Challenge of Christian Maturity," Fr. James Bacik presents Rahner's theological anthropology for an understanding of human life. The mature person is one who achieves a fruitful synthesis of opposing tendencies. The pursuit of these dialectical virtues, which represent a middle way, enables Christians to respond effectively to diverse situations and serves to guide them in their efforts to achieve genuine adulthood. In his book *The Gracious Mystery*,[2] Bacik expands on the themes of his article and offers a model for contemporary spirituality.

As I reflected on the implications of both my personal experience and Bacik's article for adult religions education, the following themes surfaced: (1) lifelong learning systems; (2) human growth and development; (3) expanding dimensions concerning ways of knowing, critical thinking, and mentoring. To consider these themes with some sense of order, I should like first to establish a particular framework, drawn from the work of Leon McKenzie.

In *The Purposes and Scope of Adult Religious Education*,[3] McKenzie offers a paradigm for organizing a system of lifelong learning based on

---

[1] Evelyn Eaton Whitehead and James D. Whitehead, *Seasons of Strength* (Garden City, N.Y.: Image Books, 1986).

[2] James J. Bacik, *The Gracious Mystery* (Cincinnati: St. Anthony Messenger Press, 1987).

[3] Leon McKenzie, "The Purposes and Scope of Adult Religious Education," *Handbook of Adult Religious Education*, Nancy Foltz, ed. (Birmingham, Ala.: Religious Education Press, 1986), pp. 10-13.

the notion that meaning is critical for human beings. He specifies meaning as

> . . . an interpretive structure or framework that defines a person's being-in-the-world and his or her existential stance toward reality. A religious framework is based on a definite faith commitment and on a set of faith affirmations and values that serve as first principles for reflection and action.[4]

Because these principles are religious rather than philosophical, they result from our response to revelatory events and imply a loving relationship with God. McKenzie, therefore, sees religious education as a process encompassing (1) the acquisition of meaning; (2) the exploration and expansion of meaning; and (3) the expression of meaning in a productive manner. The role of the adult educator is to facilitate this threefold process.

1. The Acquisition of Meaning

The initial purpose of religious education is to make available a particular meaning framework to children and neophytes in the faith community. For the individual, this foundational framework includes both knowledge and experience of the tradition. The framework functions to provide order and assists in the development of personal identity.

The need to acquire meaning is a strong argument for having lifelong learning systems, especially given several aspects of contemporary church life. One of these is that during the past twenty years, membership in the Catholic Church has grown by a solid sixteen percent.[5] Another is that the *Rite of Christian Initiation of Adults*[6] includes five variants pertaining to the various groups of catechumens and candidates. And, according to Maureen Kelly, parents who come to the Church to prepare themselves for the baptism of their child run the gamut of church affiliation from being active to being drifters, alienated, or pagans.[7] The simple fact is that with chronological maturity comes differentiation.

---

4 Ibid., p. 10.

5 See Richard N. Ostling, "Those Mainline Blues," *Time* (May 22, 1989): 94-96.

6 International Commission on English in the Liturgy, *Rite of Christian Initiation of Adults* (Washington, D.C.: USCC Office for Publishing and Promotion Services, 1988).

7 Cf. Maureen A. Kelly, "Shaping Parent Sacramental Programs for the Future," *New Catholic World* 230:1379 (September/October 1987): 202-204.

A system of lifelong learning is therefore important for accommodating all of these constituencies, whether they are acquiring an initial meaning framework or reacquiring a lost tradition. In this regard, the focus is on what best constitutes the network of learning activities and experiences that form a basic structure. In other words, how do people come to *know*?

To help adult educators gain additional insight into this question, I would like to recommend three recent resources:

- *Women's Ways of Knowing,* by Mary Field Belenky, describes "five different perspectives from which women view reality and draw conclusions about truth, knowledge and authority."[8]

- *Educating in Faith,* by Mary C. Boys, offers a "new way of thinking about what it means to educate religiously."[9] I especially recommend Part Two: "Visions."

- *Women and Teaching,* by Maria Harris, models a process of artistic knowing and maintains that it is crucial to wholistic learning.[10]

2. *The Exploration and Expansion of Meaning*

McKenzie sets forth a number of ways in which educators can help learners explore and expand initial meaning structures. He suggests (a) that learners be assisted to investigate the richness of their religious tradition and to study its nuances; (b) that they be helped to reflect on and to relate their religious tradition to their life experiences; and (c) that adolescents and adult learners be encouraged and supported to examine critically their religious tradition.

a) *The Nuances of Religious Tradition.* Initiation into the faith gives way to continuing growth on the journey with God to Christian maturity. Our religious heritage is so rich and finely nuanced that, as a subject for study, it can never be exhausted. Since Vatican II, formal programming in adult education has, in general, provided quality opportunities for deepening personal knowledge about our religious tradition. The fact that three video programs on church history have been released within the past year indicates continuing, if not grow-

---

[8] Mary Field Belenky, et al., *Women's Ways of Knowing* (New York: Basic Books, Inc., 1986).

[9] Mary C. Boys, *Educating in Faith* (San Francisco: Harper and Row, 1989).

[10] Maria Harris, *Women and Teaching* (Mahwah, N.J.: Paulist Press, 1988), see esp. ch. 4.

ing, interest in learning about our roots. I would not venture to make the same claim, however, concerning nuances. I have found many adults are relatively ignorant of shades of difference vis-à-vis their religious tradition.

b) *Relating to Life Experiences.* When educators help learners relate their religious tradition to their experiences, they provide them with opportunities to derive greater meaning from life's events and to give enhanced purpose to their living. A helpful resource for this is Dr. James Fowler's book *Faith Development and Pastoral Care,* [11] in which he identifies three broad categories of change: (1) developmental, (2) reconstructive, and (3) intrusive marker events. Developmental change results from maturation and formation of self. Reconstructive change includes "breakdown and rebuilding, restoration and healing, conversion and transformation" (p. 101). Intrusive marker events are disruptive events that irrevocably alter life's patterns.

A related resource is Nancy Foltz's book *Handbook of Adult Religious Education,*[12] in which she chronicles life-cycle patterns with program needs and advocates enhanced use of the social sciences to enable learners to forge links between tradition and life.

In *Effective Teaching and Mentoring,*[13] Laurent Daloz writes of the transformational power of adult learning experiences, delineates the qualities of the mentor, and defines three key roles: support, challenge, and vision.

In the role of *support,* the mentor confirms the learner's self-worth, affirms the validity of present experience, and assures the capacity for further growth at the appropriate time. In systems language, boundaries are brought into congruence.

The tasks of support are active listening, perspective taking (i.e., what it feels like to be this person), providing structure, expressing positive expectations, serving as advocate, and sharing self.

In the role of *challenge,* the boundaries are gently pulled apart; assumptions are questioned; tensions, calling for closure, are created. The purpose is to provide a new vision.

The functions of challenge are to set tasks, engage in discussion, heat up dichotomies, construct hypotheses, and set high standards.

In providing *vision,* the roles of the mentor are to model, to keep the tradition, to offer a map, to suggest new language, and to provide

---

[11] James W. Fowler, Ph.D., *Faith Development and Pastoral Care* (Philadelphia: Fortress Press, 1987), see esp. ch. 6 and 7.

[12] Nancy Foltz, ed., *Handbook of Adult Religious Education* (Birmingham, Ala.: Religious Education Press, 1986), ch. 3-9, pp. 59-232.

[13] Laurent A. Daloz, *Effective Teaching and Mentoring* (San Francisco: Jossey-Bass Publishers, 1987).

a mirror. Fred Eyerman proposes that "educational brokering, counseling, and spiritual direction should become more prevailing styles for adult religious educators . . . who . . . should be capable of helping individuals respond to the key experiences in their lives in dialog and tension with the Christian vision and the signs of our times."[14]

Daloz lists five steps of effective mentoring: (1) listening to the stories of the learners; (2) seeing oneself as a guide; (3) promoting development as a part of program planning; (4) creating networks of learners and facilitators who share similar concerns; and (5) recognizing that, at least in part, personal growth is an interdependent activity.

c) *Critical Examination.* Mentoring can also model a way to question constructively the religious tradition from within the institution, a task that is essential to Christian maturity. In *Developing Critical Thinkers,* Stephen Brookfield argues that to think critically is to recognize the assumptions underlying our beliefs and behaviors. Critical thinking includes two interrelated processes: identifying and challenging assumptions and imagining and exploring alternatives. It is a continuous process and includes alternating phases of:

> (1) reflecting on a problem or theme; (2) testing new solutions, strategies, or methods on the basis of that reflection; (3) reflecting on the success of these actions in particular contexts; and (4) further honing, refining, and adapting these actions according to alternative contexts.[15]

The key to the process is *thinking as action.*

Brookfield's purpose is to help learners become adept at critical thinking in four arenas central to the lives of adults: their intimate relationships, their workplaces, their political involvements, and their perception of the world as influenced by mass media.

3. The Expression of Meaning

In McKenzie's process, the third purpose of religious education is to help learners become adept at expressing meaning. In catechetical terms, this is learning for living; in ecclesial language it is mission. Learners equipped with meaning frameworks interpret situations of meaninglessness as calls for action. Believers guided by their religious

---

[14] Fred Eyerman, "Reclaiming Meaning: A Response to the Mature Christian Adult," *Agenda for the 90s: Forging the Future of Adult Religious Education* (Washington, D.C.: USCC Office for Publishing and Promotion Services, 1989), pp. 13-18.

[15] Stephen D. Brookfield, *Developing Critical Thinkers* (San Francisco: Jossey-Bass Publishers, 1987), p. 230.

convictions bring meaning to the world. Men and women rooted in the tradition, energized by prayer, and led by the Spirit live out their religious heritages in their families, in their social contexts, and in the marketplace. In educating for maturity, the Church works honestly and courageously toward a world of equality, justice, and peace.

This vision demands mature Christians: people of faith and communities of vocation and virtue. Adulthood means living in paradox and ambiguity with commitment and fidelity; initiating, exploring, expanding, and expressing the meaningfulness of human life. We are called to growth by God and self for others. We journey together.

A Contemporary Spirituality for Mature Christians

Robert F. Morneau

A week after being asked to write this article, I was attending a college board of trustees meeting. During the coffee break, I asked a fellow board member to jot down what she would consider to be characteristics of an adult spirituality in today's world. Ten minutes later I received this listing:

- a vital relationship with the Transcendent (God)
- an openness to life and to everything that that openness implies
- a profound respect for all people
- global awareness
- a humble self-confidence

A few days earlier, I had listed for myself several aspects of what I considered to be a contemporary spiritual vision:

Discernment: the ability to sort out the stirrings of God in everyday life.

Discipline: the capacity and freedom to achieve essential goals.

Dialectic: an awareness that apparent contradictory forces or ideas are often reciprocal and mutually creative.

Dialogue: the desire to listen attentively and to respond appropriately to the grace of the moment.

Docility: a flexibility in letting God's priorities and concerns replace our own.

Obedience: a commitment to whatever God asks of us.

Reflecting upon these two lists and listening to the experiences of many people who truly seek the ways of God, I would like to offer a possible theological framework for a contemporary spirituality for mature Christians. From one point of view, there is no contemporary spirituality since our life in grace is eternal and, in a sense, transcends time and space. Yet, our cultural situation and the individual ambience of each of our lives call for a unique application of general spiritual principles that remain valid in all times and places. Thus, this is a "quasi-contemporary spirituality," one that challenges us in the last years of the twentieth century to live in and respond to God's presence in a unique way.

Such a spirituality is integrative, Christological, interdependent, hopeful, creaturely, and creative.

1. *Integrative*

A contemporary spirituality demands coordinated vision: one eye on divinity, one eye on humanity.

One of the most significant documents of Vatican Council II is the *Pastoral Constitution on the Church in the Modern World* (*Gaudium et Spes*). There, the Vatican fathers express clearly and forcefully the Church's responsibilities to improve the world.

Too often a type of other-worldliness influenced various spiritual movements and individual lives in such a fashion that religion became privatized. A split occurred between one's religious commitment and the need to be involved in political, economic, social, and cultural issues that affected human dignity and solidarity.

The *Pastoral Constitution,* with great balance and clarity, presents an ecclesiology that refuses to dichotomize the Church and the world. Thus, we are a Church *in* the world, a world that God loved so much that he sent his only Son for its redemption. While demanding involvement, the document clearly does not permit the Church to be co-opted by an ideology or value system that is incompatible with the gospel.

The *Pastoral Constitution* calls for an integration of faith with the marketplace. We must take a long, loving look at suffering humankind and respond to the needs of the hurting. But also it is necessary to look lovingly into the face of mystery, the presence of our God, who is both transcendent as well as immanent. Worship is not to be replaced by a social gospel of simple human justice nor is our duty to work for the development of all peoples to displace our consciousness of the truths of Jesus' saving life and death.

Given this framework, one of the characteristics of a contemporary spirituality is to recover our sense of the sacred, of the holy, of the transcendent, both as that mystery manifests itself in everyday life as well as in contemplative prayer. Our task, through this loving attention (contemplation), is to sit in the stillness of God's love and to express our praise and thanksgiving. Such "idle resting" and selfless prayer, far from being nonpragmatic and unproductive, becomes the wellspring by which we retain our humanity and participate more deeply in God's creative and salvific designs. What will emerge from this quality time in the presence of God will be a renewed commitment to God's priorities as well as abundant energy to translate those priorities into reality. Failure to stay in touch cuts us off from the source of grace.

Two dispositions are essential here: *stillness* and *reverence.* Until the spirit is hushed, until purity of spirit is felt, we tend to be too hurried and fail to make room for the divine visitation. Until we hold sacred God's abiding presence and realize our own unworthiness, our heart will be ill-disposed to the action of grace. Such silence and awe are difficult in our contemporary culture of noise and cynicism.

Two writers capture this first characteristic: an Anglican lay woman and a Carmelite nun. Their words speak for themselves.

> Enrichment of the sense of God is surely the crying need of our current Christianity. A shallow religiousness, the tendency to be content with a bright ethical piety wrongly called practical Christianity . . . seems to be one of the defects of institutional religion at the present time. We are drifting towards a religion which consciously or unconsciously keeps its eye on humanity rather than on Deity— which lays all the stress on service and hardly any of the stress on awe, and that is a type of religion which in practice does not wear well.[1]

The House at Rest

"On a dark night
Kindled in love with yearnings—
Oh, happy chance!—
I went forth unobserved,
My house being now at rest."
(St. John of the Cross)

How does one hush one's house,
each proud possessive wall, each sighing rafter,
the rooms made restless with remembered laughter
or wounding echoes, the permissive doors,
the stairs that vacillate from up to down,
windows that bring in color and event
from countryside or town,

[1] Cf. Evenly Underhill, *An Anthology of the Love of God* (London: A. R. Mowbray & Co. Ltd., 1976), p. 123.

oppressive ceilings and complaining floors?

The house must first of all accept the night.
Let it erase the walls and their display,
impoverish the rooms till they are filled
with humble silences; let clocks be stilled
and all the selfish urgencies of day.

Midnight is not the time to greet a guest.
Caution the doors against both foes and friends,
and try to make the windows understand
their unimportance when the daylight ends.
Persuade the stairs to patience, and deny
the passages their aimless to and fro.
Virtue it is that puts a house at rest.
How well repaid that tenant is, how blest
who, when the call is heard,
is free to take his kindled heart and go.[2]

2. *Christological*

A contemporary spirituality demands a faith that actually walks the path of Jesus; an internal change of mind and heart must be followed by a life-style congruent with the gospel.

In the *Decree on the Church's Missionary Activity* (*Ad Gentes*), we read: ". . . the Church, urged on by the Spirit of Christ, must walk the road Christ himself walked, a way of poverty and obedience, of service and self-sacrifice even to death, a death from which he emerged victorious by his resurrection" (no. 5). Wherever we find these four footprints—gospel poverty, authentic obedience, gracious service, joyful self-sacrifice—we can be assured that the Lord has recently passed by. The task of every individual and community is to pursue this narrow way that leads to freedom and life.

Our culture frowns upon such values. Affluence is the ideal, not a spirit or life of radical poverty; unlimited self-determination undermines even a whisper of obedience; immediate gratification of every desire and whim turns sacrifice and service into a rather sad joke. The operative anthropology of our day asserts that self-development does not lie along the road of denial and death to self but in the fulfillment

---

[2] Jessica Powers, *The House at Rest* (Pewaukee, Wis.: Carmelite Monastery, 1984), p. 9.

of our longings and appetites. Our lexicon no longer includes the word *asceticism*, the only path that keeps us from the mire of self-indulgence.

Walking the path Christ trod contains that mysterious paradox that puzzles and confuses the human heart: life emerging from death. Our age has attempted—consciously or otherwise—to deny death and its cousin, sacrifice. Devoid of a spiritual mooring, death must be denied since it means, without faith, annihilation. This in turn renders human existence absurd and meaningless. The spiral rapidly plunges the human spirit into lethargy, if not despair.

Maturity demands sacrifice. Christian maturity demands the willingness to carry one's own cross and the burdens of others. St. Paul, who tends at times to be hyperbolic, is not so in this passage from his letter to the Galatians: "Bear one another's burdens, and so you will fulfill the law of Christ" (6:2). A contemporary novelist, Charles Williams, also cuts through to the essence of life: "You must give your burden up to someone else, and you must carry someone else's burden."[3]

The thoughts of the mind and the affections of the heart must be turned into action. Jesus not only proclaimed the kingdom of God but also lived the demands of that kingdom, a kingdom of truth and charity, of freedom and justice. Insofar as we walk that noble though narrow path, and despite the fact that at times we stumble and are lost, we demonstrate that interior conversion is authentic. Only by tracking the footprints of God as manifest in the life of Jesus will we give credible witness to a skeptical and atheistic world.

3. Interdependent

A contemporary spirituality demands that our personal relationship with God be connected to all of creation and that we assume appropriate responsibility for one another and for our universe.

The Yale psychiatrist Robert Jay Lifton begins his book *The Broken Connection* with this phrase: "We live on images." Images condition attitudes which, in turn, radically influence behavior. A central image of our century is the earthrise. Never before in human history was the earth viewed from outer space as a small, blue and grey ball—our small global village—flying through space at an incredible speed. That image has serious and practical implications: we are one family; all is interconnected; no person, country, or culture is an island.

---

[3] Cf. Charles Williams, *Descent into Hell* (Grand Rapids, Mich.: William B. Eerdmans Publishing Company, 1937), p. 99.

Illness happens when things are disconnected, separated, broken. Health, at the physical, psychological, and spiritual levels, is fostered when things are in harmonious relationship with one another. Sin is *the* broken connection. Grace is what unites and brings us into an organic whole. Spirituality has to do with union and unity. Insofar as we are one with God and united with our brothers and sisters, will peace and joy flow through life.

Thus, it should not be surprising that recent pastoral letters from the National Conference of Catholic Bishops focused on political and economic issues. Our life of faith is so interwoven with human dignity at every level that to truly live a life of grace, one must be intimately involved in the practical lives of people. A false spirituality and an incredulous Church isolate themselves from proximity to the poor, solidarity with the hurting, oneness with the marginal. We are all part of the Mystical Body of Christ, all interconnected, so that when one suffers, we all suffer; when one rejoices, we all rejoice.

Two extremes are to be avoided in a contemporary spirituality: *excessive dependency* and a *haughty independence*. The very nature of our creaturehood means that at the depth of our being we are dependent—dependent upon our ecological environment for survival; dependent upon affirmation and support for sound psychological living; dependent upon God for every stirring of grace. Needy we are, but there is also an addictive dependency that refuses to accept responsibility for our own life and well-being. To the extent that addictions reign in our lives, we are not free. The other extreme is either to go it alone, denying the need for others, or to be so turned off by human pettiness as to avoid vulnerable contact with others and with God. Its crassest form is the rampant individualism that cuts people off from the larger social units. Lacking a social consciousness and global awareness, individuals and nations seek only their self-interest without any commitment to the common good.

John Donne knew of what he spoke:

> No man is an island, entire of itself; every man is a piece of the continent, a part of the main. If a clod be washed away by sea, Europe is the less, as well as if a promontory were, as well as if a manor of thy friend's or of thine were: any man's death diminishes me, because I am involved in mankind, and therefore never send to know for whom the bell tolls, it tolls for thee.[4]

Perhaps the best entrance into a contemporary spirituality of any century is to return to the Lord's Prayer. When prayed with reverence and devotion, we touch the deep reality that God is Father of all and

---

[4] John Donne, *Devotion upon Emergent Occasions*, Meditation XVII.

that we constitute but a single, organic family. Until that prayer is experienced and not merely sung or recited, we will fail to know who we really are and what our task in life is. Jesus heals the broken connection by reconciling us once again to God and to one another. Only after that link is reforged, will peace be possible.

4. *Hopeful*

A contemporary spirituality demands that we be people of hope, having confidence in the promises of God and in the radical goodness of all life.

In an editorial in *America,* a quotation is given from the writings of Teilhard de Chardin:

> It has become fashionable today to mock or to treat with suspicion anything that looks like faith in the future. If we are not careful, this skepticism will be fatal, for its direct result is to destroy both the love of living and the momentum of mankind.[5]

Although the expression "faith in the future" is used, we know that hope, as well as faith, in the future are directly related. The warning sign indicated by Teilhard is to be taken seriously. We live in a century of incredible violence and greed. Cynicism about our political leaders, suspicions about the life-style of religious leaders, skepticism regarding our educational institutions, discouragement over the plight of the homeless and unemployed, anxieties over the ecological pollution that is destroying our fragile planet—the litany ends not in praise but in a sense of hopelessness, a hopelessness that paralyzes the human spirit.

We cannot run from the facts of human irresponsibility, from our individual and collective sins. Nor can we run from the mystery of God's providential care and love for the world that he created and redeemed through the death and resurrection of Jesus. Our hopefulness lies not in our trust of technology, progress, or human enterprises. Rather, it resides in our confidence that God is still with us and for us and that through grace we will be channels of God's truth, freedom, love, and justice in our own times. Our trust and confidence is grounded in our adherence to the indwelling Spirit, who never abandons us nor withholds the gifts that lead to deep internal renewal.

In one of the most powerful and beautifully written documents of the Church, namely, Pope Paul VI's apostolic exhortation *On Evangelization in the Modern World* (*Evangelii Nuntiandi*), we are given a faith

---

5. *America,* 159: 20, p. 530.

perspective for grounding our hope. The pope writes:

> Consequently evangelization cannot but include the prophetic proclamation of a hereafter, man's profound and definitive calling, in both continuity and discontinuity with the present situation: beyond time and history, beyond the transient reality of this world, and beyond the things of this world, of which a hidden dimension will one day be revealed—beyond man himself, whose true destiny is not restricted to his temporal aspect but will be revealed in the future life. Evangelization therefore also includes the preaching of hope in the promises made by God in the new Covenant in Jesus Christ, the preaching of God's love for us and of our love for God; the preaching of brotherly love for all [people]—the capacity of giving and forgiving, of self-denial, of helping one's brother and sister—which, springing from the love of God, is the kernel of the Gospel; the preaching of the mystery of evil and of the active search for good.[6]

For hope to be activated and sustained, God's word must be proclaimed in season and out of season. This prophetic task has taken on new urgency, given the fact that there is so much bad news in the world today, news that spreads across our planet every day through satellite communication. Modern technology can seriously threaten the gospel message when it presents only the dark side of human nature. Once again the sound of a faith-filled human voice must speak to the heart and tell of the fidelity and providence of our gracious, loving God.

5. Creaturely

> **A contemporary spirituality demands that we come to a radical acceptance of and delight in the mystery of our creaturehood and creativity.**

As a pilgrim Church, we are constantly searching for meaning and for love. Meaninglessness is equivalent to illness' lack of love, to incredible suffering. In a century where pluralism and relativism are prevalent, at a time when love is constantly threatened by violence and egoism, we must once again ask the question of who we are before the mystery of our God. Again, it might be well to listen to a contemporary poet and ponder her insights.

---

[6] Paul VI, *On Evangelization in the Modern World* (*Evangelii Nuntiandi*), (Vatican: December 8, 1975), no. 28.

To Live with the Spirit

To live with the Spirit of God is to be a listener.
It is to keep the vigil of mystery,
  earthless and still.
One leans to catch the stirring of the Spirit,
  strange as the wind's will.
The soul that walks where the wind of the Spirit blows
  turns like a wandering weather-vane toward love.
It may lament like Job or Jeremiah,
  echo the wounded heart, the mateless dove.
It may rejoice in spaciousness of meadow
  that emulates the freedom of the sky.
Always it walks in waylessness, unknowing;
  it has cast down forever from its hand
  the compass of the whither and the why.
To live with the Spirit of God is to be a lover.
It is becoming love, and like to Him
  toward Whom we strain with metaphors of creatures:
  fire-sweep and water-rush and the wind's whim.
The soul is all activity, all silence;
  and though it surges Godward to its goal,
  it holds, as moving earth holds sleeping noonday,
  the peace that is the listening of the soul.[7]

Two things define our creaturehood: being *listeners* and *lovers*. Through the virtue of obedience, we listen to the mystery of our God as revealed in Jesus, the Church and the sacraments, Scripture and nature; through the virtue of charity, we strive to live loving lives that are characterized by justice and peace.

Obedience and charity confront some formidable foes. Both our culture and our deep instinctual drives urge upon us the attainment of security, esteem, and power. Obedience and discipline are seen as incompatible with human freedom; trust and love as naive in a world of war and avarice. When presented with the mystery of our creaturehood and the call to service, the immediate tendency is to cry out: "I will not serve!" From the Christian perspective, not to serve in obedience and love, not to be a listener and a lover is to miss what life is all about.

---

[7] Jessica Powers, *The House at Rest*, p. 68.

6. *Creative*

A contemporary spirituality demands that we be open and responsive to the call to be creative.

There is another mystery that we must also be vigilant about in our search for a contemporary spirituality, namely, the call to creativity. Our God is a life-giver, and every person is called to be creative. What must be discerned is one's own giftedness, for it is through that grace that God makes us to be instruments of peace and life to others. Some exercise their creativity as teachers; others as parents, healers, or administrators. Not to develop one's creativity is to deny something so basic as to risk losing a sense of one's own identity. Yet with the gift comes a serious responsibility: to use the gift in building up the common good and furthering the work of the kingdom. Fear of that responsibility or want of discipline in its development leaves many people with a sense of emptiness and futility.

Creativity furthers God's creative design and provides us with a sense of ultimate purpose. A certain glory is manifest as we allow God to reveal his goodness through our personhood. Paradoxically, it may happen that through suffering and weakness God's glory will have a special brilliance. Creativity is not just a matter of positive achievements in the sharing of life. It is also visible when individuals are powerless in their diminishment and misery. All things can work unto good for those who love God.

Conclusion

Perhaps the greatest need we have in our search for a contemporary spirituality is *witness*. We need to be able to see individuals and communities who actually live the gospel story. The call is to discipleship, one that is simple, humble, and faithful. It is clear from our teaching that the universal vocation is a call to holiness. That is something that must be responded to not only in the streets of Calcutta, but at the kitchen tables of our homes and in the halls of our legislatures. Christ, present and manifest, is what spirituality is all about.

But the living of this life is essentially a gift. The Spirit of Jesus and the Father has been offered to us. We must daily pray that our minds and hearts be open to this uncreated grace. Again, a poem captures this desire and draws us into the heart of every spirituality, old and new.

Come, South Wind

"By south wind is meant the Holy Spirit who awakens love."
(St. John of the Cross)

Over and over I say to the south wind: come,
  waken in me and warm me!
I have walked too long with a death's chill in the air,
  mourned over trees too long with branches bare.
Ice has a falsity for all its brightness
  and so has need of your warm reprimand.
A curse be on the snow that lapsed from whiteness,
  and all bleak days that paralyze my land.

I am saying all day to Love who wakens love:
  rise in the south and come!
Hurry me into springtime; hustle the winter
  out of my sight;
  make dumb the north wind's loud impertinence.
Then plunge me into my leafing and my blossoming,
  and give me pasture, sweet and sudden pasture.
Where could the Shepherd bring his flocks to graze?
Where could they rest at noonday?
O south wind, listen to the woe I sing!
One whom I love is asking for the summer
  from me, who still am distances from spring.[8]

[8] Ibid., p. 13.

Participating in the Holy: Challenges for a Twenty-First Century Church

Jack McBride

I have always appreciated Bishop Robert Morneau's friendship with both the written and the spoken word. He possesses the pastoral good sense to draw upon consistently the wisdom of the community for verse and story. As a result, both he and his ministerial style are pastorally eclectic and spiritually expressive.

In reflecting on Bishop Morneau's article, I wish first to lay some groundwork in definition and context and then to draw some implications for church leadership.

Definition and Context

The holy is, as Bishop Morneau states, eternal; it transcends time and space. Spirituality is our way of participating in the holy; it is a matter of relationship, of connectedness. We are connected with God, the cosmos, our ancestors, those now living and future generations. Spirituality is also a matter of unavoidable risk. The risk occurs when we allow ourselves either to touch or to be touched by the holy. It also occurs when we choose to ignore the holy. Risk, then, is a constant whose outcome will be either liberation or smothering self-indulgence.

Contemporary spirituality entails having a charismatic appreciation of life. It necessitates developing an ability to let go of our need for control and allowing ourselves to be surprised by the Spirit, by the unexpectedness of the holy.

It is the unexpectedness of the holy that catches us up short, that rouses us from our everyday routine, that empowers the least likely of us and lays low those we esteem.

Spirituality, then, may be less of a dialogue with the holy than a dance with it. The music of the dance is determined to a large extent by the context of the times. For example, there was a time when the society in which our ancestors' danced was orientated to authoritarianism and organized according to a strict hierarchical order legitimated by religious consecration.[1]

---

[1] For further discussion of modernity and social and religious organization refer to an occasional paper by Joe Holland, *The Spiritual Crisis of Modern Culture* (Washington, D.C.: The Center of Concern, 1984).

Now, as we come to the close of the twentieth century, to what social analysts call the modern era, we have seen our society and, in the last twenty years, our Church oriented to a "professionalism" that is defined most often by the number of academic degrees one possess rather than by the identification of useful skills. The "music" for this modern orientation derives its legitimacy from the alluring, yet somewhat fuzzy standards of "secular professional competency."

As we move into the twenty-first century, the music will change again and so will the dance. There are signs that the post-modern society and the post-modern Church will place less emphasis on professionalism than on gifted participation. *Community* will become the key form of organization, governed by creative imagination and legitimated primarily by the discernment of charisms. The legitimating criterion of charism will keep the Church on its toes as the music plays. (We caught a glimpse of this during the brief waltz of Pope John XXIII). Thus, consecration and competence will no longer be the exclusive legitimating criteria. Rather, they will be honored as important dimensions at the service of the community. "What is Apollos, after all, and what is Paul? Ministers through whom you became believers, just as the Lord assigned each one" (1 Cor 3:5).

The holy challenges us to new ways of thinking and doing. This is why a spirituality based on the unchartered nature of the holy involves risks. Participating in the holy demands that we recognize four immediate challenges for the church leadership: (1) trust, affirm, and enable the community; (2) confront our excuses; (3) change our methods; and (4) evaluate our formation practices.

1. Trust, Affirm, and Enable the Community

Community ought to be the operant form of the Church. Estrangement between clergy and laity, men and women, young and old, rural and city must be healed. We are all *laos*—one people of God. As a people, we are all part of that crossbeam on the continuum of time, gifted at conception and called by name in baptism by Jesus, who is the intersecting point. Instead of accentuating a hierarchy of roles, post-modern spirituality will enjoy a heightened appreciation of charism. Roles will not as easily define persons and dictate dispositions. Rather, personhood, which is called forth and empowered by the community, will inform role (cf. 1 Cor 12:12-31).

The Church of the late-twentieth century and beyond will need to act on its belief that the universe and all people are imbued with the spirit of God. Although discernment of the spirit is continually necessary, the *sensus fidelium* must be taken more seriously by the entire Church, including those of us who serve as professionals in church ministry. In other words, we must be more trusting of those we serve. Trust affirms, enables, and empowers. Trust does not condescend, manipulate, or demand. Trust and reconciliation build up a community. As Bishop Morneau suggests, *integration* and *interdependence* will be two of the pillars that the spirituality of the Church will rest upon. But how will these efforts be measured? "[T]he fruit of the Spirit is love, joy, peace, patience, kindness, generosity, faithfulness, gentleness, self-control. . . . If we live in the Spirit, let us also follow the Spirit" (Gal 5:22,25). How do our parish, diocesan, and national church communities measure up next to the fruits of the Spirit?

2. Confront Our Excuses

Bishop Morneau warns us that cynicism and complaints easily give way to hopelessness, and hopelessness can paralyze the human spirit. Consequently, obstacles must become opportunities. The church community of which we speak will be governed by "creative imagination."

The three most common excuses used to put the Spirit on hold in dioceses and parishes are (1) our parish is too large and impersonal; (2) we're just a small parish with no staff and no budget and; (3) the people are apathetic. Holding each of these excuses up to the light of the gospel, let us begin with Jesus' feeding the 5,000 strangers in Mark 6:34-44. Jesus gathered the "congregation" together when he preached, but he later broke them down into smaller groups so they could participate and be nourished. We must follow Jesus' example: large is too large if we expect to realize a "participatory community". Our church populations (large and small) must be broken down into smaller, more intimate communities.[2]

Jesus also seemed undaunted by his small "congregation," lack of staff, and low budget. He simply worked with what he and his "congregation" had—an overflow of charism. He improvised. He used nature and life's experience and invited people to recognize that all of life, both the mundane and the sublime, is revelatory. Jesus also empowered members of his "congregation."

Jesus affirmed people's charisms and enabled them to serve the community. He did not hesitate out of fear that they would make mistakes—which they did. He was not paranoid that they would say the wrong thing; Peter certainly did. As a matter of fact, Jesus so

---

[2] For further suggestions and encouragement see Arthur R. Baranowski, *Creating Small Faith Communities* (Cincinnati: St. Anthony Messenger Press, 1988); Michael A. Cowan and Bernard Lee, *Dangerous Memories: House Churches and Our American Story* (New York: Sheed and Ward, 1986).

empowered the members of his "congregation" that even they were surprised. Recall the return of the seventy-two in Luke 10:17-20.

Jesus countered apathy peripatetically, that is, he walked around. Not long ago my friend, Grandma Henryka was telling me how common it is to see the parish priests in Poland walking around the neighborhood. (We have a pope who employs the same pastoral approach). Henryka wondered why more American priests do not do the same. Do we expect the people to come to us, to our church office, our parish hall, our diocesan center, or do we get out, walk around, and meet people *where they are*? This question ought to be pondered by all of us who work in church ministry.

Apathy occurs when people are not engaged, or when needs remain unknown or unmet. As a Church, we need to employ processes that more accurately assess people's needs. For a generation, our program planning has steadily improved in the areas of adult education, community service, and social integration. However, the most severe hunger stems from spiritual malnourishment. In 1988, *Better Homes and Gardens* published a survey entitled "Are Americans Finding New Strength in Spirituality?"[3] An overwhelming 80,000 readers responded. People are spiritually hungry, and they can tell us exactly how they would like to be nourished if only we would find ways to ask them. Are we asking them?

3. Change Our Methods

We must risk not only being more creative but also affirming the creative in the community. We simply have been relying too much on "Father," the staff, and the so-called experts whom we import.

Bishop Morneau emphatically observes that a "contemporary" spirituality *demands* that we be open and responsive to the call to be creative. Jesus never stifled creativity; he recognized it when friends lowered the paralyzed man through the roof (cf. Lk 5:17-26) or when Zacchaeus climbed the sycamore tree to catch a glimpse of Him (cf. Lk 19:1-9).

We must not be slaves to conventional methods that promote only "professional doer roles" that serve grateful "receivers." Creativity needs to be an operational principle for our Church as it moves into the twenty-first century. Our post-modern Church will spend more effort identifying the charisms and skills within our congregations. Just imagine the benefit to our community if we had the same knowledge

---

[3] Refer to the information on "Narrow Casting Needs Assessment" from the leadership training program entitled, *Priming the Pump*. Tabor Publications, 1988.

of our members' gifts and skills as we do of their yearly monetary contributions.

Yet, simply recognizing those gifts and skills is not sufficient. Bishop Morneau warns us that with each gift comes the serious responsibility to build up "the common good" of the community. Discernment leads to knowledge, and knowledge must lead to empowerment. The members of our future congregations will not only live with a clearer understanding of their gifts and skills but will also enthusiastically offer their charisms in service to the community. A grand collaboration of charisms will be at the service of the local, diocesan, and universal Church. There will be fewer experts and more recognized charisms.

We cannot wait for someday. What are we doing today to recognize and empower both the gifts and skills of every member of our church community?

4. Evaluate Our Formation Practices

"... for a person will reap only what he sows" (Gal 6:7).

According to a recent report by the Lilly Endowment, three separate researchers (Hoge, Hemrick, and Schuth) discerned that diocesan seminarians tend to be more "institutional" than "communal." The studies indicate that diocesan seminarians

> ... see themselves as set apart, distant, and separate from the laity, and as witnesses to them.... On the other hand, seminarians who are members of religious orders tend to be "communal." They show an interest in collaborating and sharing functions with the laity.[4]

The question for both clergy and professional church ministers (diocesan directors, parish directors of religious education, pastoral ministers, liturgists, etc.) therefore becomes: Are our future leaders being trained in an ecclesiology and a spirituality that foster the multiplicity of charisms inherent in our church communities? As we move into the twenty-first century, both the environment and the content of formation programs must be scrutinized to ensure an ecclesiology and a spirituality that foster true community development.

According to a 1986 study by the Vatican Congregation for Catholic Education, an overwhelming percentage of rectors and presidents told researcher Schuth that "one of the most positive impacts on the

---

[4] Jane Redmond, ed., *Progressions: A Lilly Endowment Occasional Report* 1:2 (June 1989): 14.

quality of programs for priestly formation was the presence of lay students and faculty, including women. . . ."[5] Even so, the report favored seminarians taking courses apart from the laity and having their spiritual direction provided by ordained clergy rather than by lay professionals, including women religious.

To again look to Jesus for inspiration, we are reminded that he formed the apostles in the midst of the community. The apostles were not called to isolation but to integration. Formation focused on spiritual development. In story or at gatherings, Jesus taught his apostles to pay attention to life and to people because they were the vehicles of God's revelation. The apostles and disciples were educated in the midst of the community for service to the community. The community was an instrument of learning, not of distraction. Consequently, after Jesus' death and resurrection, the apostles were better able to employ their gifts at the service of this "familiar" community. They were also better able to deal with conflict in the community because they were not isolated from it but, rather, part of it.

Two questions remain to be considered: (1) How might the formation of professional ministers (clergy and lay) be more fully integrated into the community? and (2) How can we better provide for the formation of the "nonprofessional," gifted members of our communities who wish to share their charisms?

We have explored only a few of the challenges facing us as we move into the twenty-first century. Bishop Morneau's article concludes with a clear call to bear witness to the holiness in which we participate. Our honesty in wrestling with the challenges facing our Church is the first ingredient of that faithful witness.[6]

---

[5] Ibid., p. 14.

[6] For a dose of honesty, read Mitch Finley, "Confessions of a Modern Catholic Layman," *America* 160:15 (April 22, 1989).

Clothed in Strength and Seasoned, She Flourishes

Ann Johnson

While no published developmental studies currently exist that examine maturity among women of faith, the scriptural models are abundant and telling. The working definition I offer here identifies a mature woman of faith as "one who accepts herself as Woman, made in the image of God, and lives by that definition." The paradigm I have developed focuses on four biblical life-expressions whereby we understand ourselves as Woman "like unto the One Alone." They are *Child, Kin, Helper,* and *Creator.*

As a Christian, a follower of Jesus of Nazareth, I center my thinking on womanly maturity in the prayer and biblical texts we know to have been foundational to Jesus and the disciples.

Each life-expression calls forth maturity in its own particular dimension. Maturing is not a passive process similar to aging but, rather, is quite intentional. Maturity is our promise, our joy, our gift, and our destiny. We are called to seek and to find. While we accumulate events in the passing of our days, it is the experiences lived deeply and remembered that become the blueprint of our maturity.

Experiences (both those that seem to happen to us and those that we seem to make happen) are often expressed in visceral terms: *gut-wrenching, heart-breaking, mind-bending, side-splitting, stunning.* We trust these experiences. We trust our "knowing." We are empowered according to the transforming potential articulated in God's command, "Be you as I Am."

This Godliness, or maturity, is expressed in many scriptural synonyms: *unshakable, set firm, powerful, ever-fruitful, rock, holy,* to name a few.

The forms of the feminine maturation paradigm, namely, Child, Kin, Helper, and Creator are not stages, hierarchical imperatives, journeys, or sequential processes. Though some events are age-related, none are time-specific. None are ever left behind. Growth is a trajectory. Accessible. Valid all along its beam. A Woman does not lose touch with her childliness, turn away from kinship, wait until her later years for universal ethical responsibility, or delay creative synergy.

Perhaps the scriptural symbol for maturation most available to us is that of clothing. Hebrew Scriptures and Christian Testaments speak of "donning the garb of God" or "putting on garments of the faithful." Like a loving artisan, God makes clothing for Adam and Havah (Eve) as they leave their enclosure and enter the world. God, too, is psalmodized as robed in spiritual garb.

Clothed in wonder, YHWH [Yahweh] reigns!
Putting on the garment of knowledge,
girded about with strength.
Thus the world is set firm and cannot be shaken.
(Psalm 93)

Let us now look at the four "garments" of maturity.

1. Child

Creation eagerly awaits our becoming. In the latter weeks of womb-time our personalities make themselves known to those who watch and witness our coming to birth. As children we receive, record, and remember through every fiber of our being. Sensually, urgently, we strive to taste, touch, see, hear, encounter, smell, and articulate every wonder in the created world.

As Daughters of God, we begin in childhood an apprenticeship in the wonder and "awe-full-ness" of creation, the blessedness and cursedness of loving people; the joy and pain of our bodies; the choice-making, which is our charism; the experiences of heritage and responsibility. In these precious ways, we clarify who we are from our experience.

A Time for Planting

Think of this Child-time as a season of prayer, of *T'fillah*. The Hebrew, *T'fillah*, means to clarify, to discern, to judge for oneself. In the way of children, we ask vital questions: How? Where? What? Who? When? Why? Through questioning, we are endowed with our sacred heritage: "hovered over," caressed in the palm of God's hand, breathed alive.

I have a vivid memory of my youngest daughter, Hannah. She was nine years old, and we were in the midst of a move that tore our hearts. We alternated between tears and tight efficiency.

Hannah hummed about the unfamiliar house, making settled places here and there. "Mom," she called out to me, "be careful of the stone steps. I've just moved one of the rocks to put my message there."

I was curious, and approached her.

"Is it something you can share, Hannah?"

"I don't think so."

"Okay," I said and, disappointed, turned away.

"Well, maybe I could share it because I'm bigger now. I wrote a note for myself a long time ago when I first learned to write. I wrapped it up and put it under a stone in the garden wall. Whenever I got mad at you, or sad, or had a fight, I used to go and read it. It made me feel better. Then, later, just remembering it was there became enough, and I didn't have to read it every time. So I thought I'd better move my note with me to the new house, just in case. You can look at it if you want. I put it under the stone on the edge of the porch."

I went out, sat still for a while, aware that she had shared a very special part of her secret self with me. Then I moved the obviously loose rock and saw the worn, softly seamed note beneath. Its primitive and young printing said: "God loves Hannah and Hannah loves God."

I wept and gave thanks for this sign of maturity from the youngest among us! Her simple clarity had met fear, anger, and sadness and steadied her like the rock atop her message.

A Time for Uprooting What Has Been Planted

As maturing women, we engage holy childhood as a way of life. We remember in our very bones the experiences of confusion, misunderstandings, deep hurts, despair—even woundedness. Sometimes the wounds are permanent, and we continue to bear scars; but they are not a rationale for immaturity.

In maturing, we clarify our childhood, setting it in proper relief. Thus, we forgive; we test reality; we reframe, renurture, and, yes, even rebirth in a new spiritual and psychological context. This uprooting helps us encounter anew the command to "honor our father and mother." And in so doing, we dare to live in a deeper relationship with our beloved *Abbah.*

In garbing ourselves in the season of childhood, we learn some essential lessons: Fix what is broken; not everything can be fixed. Some things are precious beyond their apparent value. Store away what you've outgrown. Bury what is dead. Clean up your mess; help others clean up their's. Hold hands so you don't get lost. Call home. Truth is easier than lies.

Jesus teaches us to come to "life" as children do. Watch them in their holy times. They awake with zest, sleep in trust. They are easily hurt, but quick to heal. They are bereft at betrayal and abandonment, yet forgiving and forgetful of wrongs done. They are fragile of body and worthy of protection. They are fierce in love, sorrow, and curiosity. They are attentive to the taste of mud, the welfare of sparrows. They care for another's despair and are authentically terror-stricken at blood, bombs, and chaos. They are rageful at the smallest injustice. They are hardy of laughter and delicious to touch.

In maturing, we gather the essence of our childhood and put it on, wearing it like an intimate garment next to the skin.

2. *Kin*

We are a people of covenant. We have opportunities to covenant ourselves consciously and carefully with our own bodies / souls, with God, with others.

Biologically, creation is eager for what we will be. By the age of ten, we often have long, fast-growing feet, as though they are anticipating the body soon to stretch above. As women, our womb comes alive soon after, bonding us with the universe in moon tides, and with all generations of potent birth-givers. Our womb comes alive and blood speaks its own mystery as we pay loving attention to our bodies, so wonder-filled with promise.

The Hebrew Scriptures retain the belief of the matriarchs in the sacredness of menses. The teachings on women's mysteries are often referred to as a "Hedge of Roses," celebrating both the time of re-entering the hedged garden (Eden) for sacred separation and the first rose-like spot of menstrual blood on clean linen.

Biblical tradition tells of a liberated Israel so bonded during the wilderness years that the entire universe together with fertile women experienced menses at a similar time, "as the moon was entering its dark phase." The women retreated together for seven days of privacy, rest, prayer, storytelling, and women's rituals. The remaining community entered into days of spiritual renewal.

Returning with the first sign of the new moon, heralded by the enkindling of holy light, the blast of the *shofar* (ritual ram's horn), the entire community celebrated the "return" in spirit, soul, and body. All participated in ritual renewal: washing, clean garments, dancing, psalmody, feasting, remembering their sacred saga.

One aspect of our maturing as adult women of faith is knowing ourselves as authentically grounded in the earth, the heavens, and in one another. When we claim as holy our physicalness, we celebrate those same essences in God, in whose likeness we are created.

Secure in our womanliness, we also open the way toward spiritual manliness. As likeness of God, we are manly, too.

Scribes recording the books of Maccabees tell of the courageous woman, mother of seven martyred sons, whose clear declaration of faith in the mystery of eternal life is the foundational theological statement on resurrection in the Scriptures. The inscribers speak of her as "valiant woman of manly soul," as mother and patriarch, as mother with the heart of Abraham.

The myriad aspects and events flowing from our sexuality open opportunities that deepen and define our sacred likeness and cause us to celebrate God with warmth and pleasure.

And so as adult women, we garb ourselves consciously, carefully. We put on covenants through which we mature in love with all our hearts, with all our minds, and with all our strength. We do not mature in isolation. The very word covenant indicates centeredness in the One Alone.

I see four categories of covenantal relationship of maturing women of faith:

1. *Personal.* This is the covenant between our public-self and the spirit-self deep within. A messenger of the Beloved, the spirit-self whispers, "ethics," "justice," "kindness," "forgive," "repair", "renew," "forget," "heal." When we fail to make this covenant, we find ourselves saying things such as, "I've got to get it together," or "I feel scattered and crazy." This covenant is foundational. With it, we are bound with the living God.

2. *Peer.* These are covenants we make with "neighbors." In the Bible, the original language has two words for neighbor. First, there is the one who dwells near or next to us, whether house to house, city to city, or border to border. Second, there is the particular neighbor, spoken of in Exodus 4, with whom we share an indwelling of spirit akin to the indwelling spirit-neighborliness of God, which is called *Shechinah.* Within these covenants, our gospel commitment to the stranger, the sojourner, and the enemy find fruitful expression.

3. *Partners.* These are covenants we make with those with whom we bind ourselves in an intentional, sacred bond where spirit-fed intimacy and fidelity ripen.

4. *The Little Ones.* These are covenants that we make with children and with those who are vulnerable. Maturity requires of us not only birth at any cost, but nurture, support, affirmation, teaching, loving, celebrating, witness, and *Shalom.* "Teach the things to your children," the Scriptures command. And, "Allow the little children to come to me, for of such is the reign of heaven." Maturity requires us to set a clearly marked path for those who follow us in order that they, too, may make their Way to the Most High.

A Time for Keeping

Think of Kin-making as a season of Scripture, of *Torah.* In Hebrew, *Torah* means to learn, to teach, the Way, to hear and do. In Scripture we learn about binding and separating. Think of Sarah's choice as she raises up the first generation of Israel. Think of Jacob, who limps forever after wrestling with the "stranger" on the night between his covenant with Laban and his reconciliation with Esau. Think of Rebecca's anguish; of Joseph's dreams; of Aaron, Miryam, and Moses; of Rahab, Tamar, Esther, Ruth, Naomi, and Mary. There are sustenance and strength to be gained from keeping our ancestors firmly before us in their binding and separating in the name of God.

A Time to Discard

Maturity also calls for us to distance ourselves from that which violates authentic adult kinship: rigidity, laziness, outmoded definitions, and outrageous expectations. This is true even with those with whom there was once warmth but now only ice. As a wise old woman told me when I was young, "Dearie, you have to know when to hang on and when to let go." The pain of discarding is a portion of this covenantal clothing.

As beloved of God, we learn to love. As neighbor, friend, and companion, we become neighborhood, community, and family. As betrothed, mother, daughter, grandmother, and sister we are kin of the Most High. As stewards of little ones, we love the "apple of God's eye."

An ancient prayer still prayed in Judaism sets the image:

YHWH [Yahweh], You have loved us
with a great and faithful love.
With deep compassion You have cared for us.
Remembering the generations who trusted in You,
we learn from You the laws of life. . . .
You have chosen us and brought us close to You
that we might show gratitude and unity in love.
Blessed are You, who has loved us
with an everlasting tenderness and chosen us in love.

3. Helper

Creation seems to await the particular person that we are. Much as we knock at the window of the householder until we are answered, so the Householder of the Universe seems to knock at the window of our soul until we turn around and embrace that sacred work to which we are appointed and for which we are uniquely gifted.

Woman as a separate entity is created as an *ezer,* a helper. Spiritual teachings employ "helper" in the same sense as *Torah* is to prayer and prayer to *Torah,* namely, one an *ezer* to the other. Scripturally, both God and Woman are called *ezer*—"helper."

I often think of this particular garment of maturity as the "robe of professionalism." There comes a time, early or late in our years, when we recognize that particular labor that enlivens us, girds our core with sacred power, and endows life with meaning. Often—indeed, usually—this gift is evident from childhood.

The discipline to bring forth our special gift of helper must be acquired, practiced. The situation, for its commencement, awaits the potent moment, the sacred situation when, prepared, we begin and accomplish.

Not a story goes by in the lives of our ancestors without that moment, that anointing, being recorded. For example, Havah (Eve) completes the image of Living Beings as God intended of us when she responds to the subtle questions stirring within her. Breaking out of naivete, she enters into the dangerous ethos of "knowing." From the beginning, the Beings are "formed" differently than the beasts. They, alone, are formed in the "Living Image," becoming creatures of both heaven and earth. They, alone, are beings formed with a capacity for choice.

And She, She from that original self was "builded" in the hands of God. Yet more to her has been added as God "builds" her essence, separate from the other one. Tradition tells of the Maker so delighted with the woman standing whole and healthy in the sacred Presence that YHWH caresses and plays with her. It is said, "And YHWH 'braided' Havah's hair." The Hebrew roots for *build* and *braid* are the same. In ancient times, even today, the bread of the Sabbath table, the *challah,* is braided in various glorious designs, ropes, and crowns to remind us of God's delight in Woman.

It is this completed Being, Woman, who fulfills the holy intention of helper and takes upon herself the labor of creation. She responds to her passion for wisdom, claims it, and shares it. In so doing, she dares to awaken to the full knowledge of her creative potential.

She, in companionship with the male with whom she is covenanted, "knows" abundance and adversity. She, with him, looks fully conscious upon creation's capacity for goodness and for evil. Inherent in the eating of the fruit of sacred knowledge is the vision of earthquake terror and rainbow blessing, of murder and birthing, of famine and harvest, of lechery and fidelity. Inherent in the eating of the fruit of sacred knowledge is the hopeful expectation that, in seeing, we will know and choose goodness. Only then are Man and Woman fit to be like God in their capacity to create living beings like themselves.

It is this "choice-maker," this "helper," that the mature woman of Spirit, the woman braided/builded in YHWH's creative expectation, becomes.

Having made our choice, we stand in awe in the Living Presence of the Beloved, we listen and understand the labor before us. Like Eve and her mate, we accept the loving attention of the One who clothes us carefully in hand-crafted garments that are made for us alone, and we go out to begin our creative labors. The Scriptures tell us Havah and Adam bore fruit quickly, a sign of blessing. Havah then offers the first prayer of wonder and gratitude in our scriptural heritage. Thus, Woman is the founder of the prayer of gratitude.

A Time for Building

Think of "help-full-ness" as a time for doing justice, of *T'zedacha*. As seasoned, maturing women, we remember God's original intent. We envision and work toward an age when God's will is done "on earth as it is in heaven," an Eden, a "Delight" for all the Living.

In Hebrew, the word for justice, *T'zedacha*, is sometimes read *righteousness*; never *charity*. Charity is that for which gratitude is expected. Charity places the receiver beneath the giver, tainting the act for both. The spirit of Jesus' expectation that those with two cloaks will share one with those who have none is a teaching of justice, not charity.

Think of "help-full-ness" as a season of kindness, of *Hesed*. This is the time to be image of God complete. A time to be kind.

Both themes emerge from ancient teachers. They say it like this: "Upon three things does the Reign of God rest in this world: upon Prayer (*T'fillah*), upon the Teaching (*Torah*), upon Righteousness (*T'zedacha*)." And from another sage: "The foundation of God's sovereignty is built on these three: prayer, walking the Way, and kindness." Or from Micah: "It is enough to love justice, do kindness and walk humbly with God."

A Time for Throwing Stones Away

As seasoned women, we cast away fantasy for what is real. We let go of rigid ideas of servanthood and chosenness. We let go false witness and themes no longer relevant. We let go of the fear of wisdom and the belief that we are "fallen-down" and cannot rise. We simply stop the "hyper-busy-ness" that quells our God-bound energy.

As we exhibit the vision and the fortitude of those wise women of our heritage who insisted that God's kindness is a lived reality, we become available to be that which is lifted up. We become fitted for that scriptural designation of the spiritually mature woman whom others recognize as "fair to look upon." We refuse to rationalize pain and sorrow, hunger and weaponry, arrogance and waste.

As Christian women we live in the post-Holocaust age, in the deadly cloud of Nagasaki and Hiroshima, in the only democracy to retain the death penalty.

As God has prophesied for us in Eden, full adulthood in the holy image demands wisdom. Like God, we enter into agony in bringing forth earth's children in behalf of the world. And in the face of it all, like God, we long for a just rule on earth and continue to bear life hopefully.

4. Creator

And the Elohim said, "Let us create Adamah, Beings of Earth, in Our own image, like unto ourselves and in their wisdom they shall be stewards of all creatures of the sea and the heavens, the earth and the swarmers upon the earth."

And you, Elohim created earth-beings in Your own image. Just like You, man and woman, You created us.

And You blessed us saying "Be fruitful and multiply, filling the earth and cherishing it. Be caretakers of the fish of the sea, the birds of heaven, and all the living creatures that move on earth."

All creation expectantly awaits that moment when we recognize "who we are," return faithful to the Image in whose likeness we are created, and claim our authentic heritage.

"For now we see into the mirror darkly, but then face to face." This natal moment is our sacred maturity. It cannot wait for old age. Here we realize that we are not on a journey or in a cycle. We are an Image, a Likeness. We are Child, Kin, Helper, and Creator all at once and over all our span. Like rain that falls on hovel and mansion alike, maturing possibilities reign in all ages of life. Whatever our age or our condition, we can reach out and with cupped hands gather in the rain to drink and offer drink. We can also let it run away unused, in rivulets of erosion. We can dig wells and plan irrigation systems to sustain life, or we can waste the rain, complaining of its inconvenience in our busy lives.

Creation, patient and hopeful, waits upon us, evening and morning, balanced, pulsing, poised upon the edge of our intention, yet to be fulfilled. Creation watches for us, witnesses our labors, remembers our efforts, records our sorrows, applauds our accomplishments, welcomes our gratitude.

It is often in steady, patterned work or rhythmic movement that we happen upon our vision. Often in dreams or diaries, our fertility bursts forth beneath our skin and startles us awake. Often in familiar ritual or in artistic creativity, we find ourselves awash with power simply to be claimed. Often in lovemaking or forgiveness, our heart breaks open in the perfect sacrifice.

And it is not just birthing we are called to. Like our Likeness we must create, sustain, support.

A Time to Gather

Think of this as the season of Salvation. Think of this as the time of Being in the Presence of God. Like God, we hover over the wild and the waste, gathering it in, separating its portions, witnessing, naming. We set spinning those new and daring dynamics never before imagined and judge them. Hovered over, we become hoverers. "O Jerusalem, how I would gather you under my wing."

Ready, we stand knowingly in the Living Presence. Oh, there are times when we cry, "Come, Lord" to one who seems remote. Or in the midst of life's rattle, we plead for greater evidence. The daily prayer of Judaism, which Jesus, Mary, and the followers prayed, cries out with confidence: "Resonate, O Presence, and your watching people will hear you and serve you in perfect service."

Living fully in the Presence of YHWH, we live expectantly as partners in the promise of sustenance and salvation. Working wonders, we come full circle to that only intuited before. In delight, we build and braid new helpers, thirsting for wisdom in our time.

Trusting, we endure. Even in experiencing jealousy and violence at the very altar of God, as did Eve with her children, we remember and continue.

A Time to Root Out

Maturity requires the rooting out of arrogance. Creative power is humbling. In creativity, there are no stereotypes. No one of us defines another. The universe speaks its own desires.

Maturity requires the rooting out of alienation. Love can be evoked and awakened, never taught. But this is a mystery of heart to heart and eye to eye.

Maturity requires the rooting out of cynicism, the putting on of love.

And so, clothed in readiness and wonder, clothed in gratitude, we develop, we mature, we ripen, we seed and are seeded, we multiply, we nurture, sustain, save. We are a vital portion of this world, feeling it all and leaving no thing unwitnessed. Barefoot, earth-stained, bloodied hands, clean, breath-filled, celebrating, we insist amidst all evidence that life is good and God is kind.

Maturity is real life witness. Maturity is a woman's joy. Laboring and resting, we are fulfilled. Accepting ourselves as Living Images of God and living by that definition, we are clothed in strength and seasoned. We flourish. We become the mature lovers we are destined to be. With Edna St. Vincent Millay, who recorded her own awakening to spiritual maturity at nineteen in her poem *Renascence,* we acknowledge, "God, I can push the grass apart and lay my finger on Thy heart."

Rummaging through Maturity

Alice Stefaniak

As I read "Clothed in Strength and Seasoned, She Flourishes" by Ann Johnson, I recognized that the images she explored were fundamental mythic images of womanhood. I savored and explored her reflections and intuitively felt that women's maturity is often like an array of life possessions tucked away in the attic. At times, society does not open the attic to notice the beauty that is there, available for anyone who ventures within.

Johnson's article initiated for me a meditative rummaging through the veritable richness of women's life stories, which I have come to share with others on my own journey.

I strongly felt that merely giving my response to the article was insufficient. So the following pages include my reflections as well as a process whereby women, in particular, can image their own maturation.

During my work with women, I have been particularly fascinated by those ranging in age from their mid-thirties into their fifties. Perhaps the reason for this is my own experience of mid-life; in any case, I know that I always feel drawn to explore the maturity questions that burgeon around those years.

Recently, I was thinking about this topic while sitting at a Canadian adult religious education conference in Ottawa. I was part of a process group called "Female and Male Perspectives in Adult Religious Education." The facilitators led us through many activities and gave us wonderful input on the faith development of both sexes. But one exercise seemed more relevant to me than the others. (And it connected to the four images of Ann Johnson). I am going to repeat it for you below because you might enjoy doing the exercise as well.

The facilitator asked us to think of our lives in six chapters or six dimensions. Each of us was to think of words, symbols, or phrases that captured the six aspects of our life from birth to the present.

List six words, symbols, or phrases that capture the six chapters of your life.

What emerged in my own reflections were six symbols: (1) a golden child; (2) exposed film; (3) a train going along on a railroad track; (4) a field in the wilderness; (5) the womb; and (6) a spiral or star.

When I was finished with the reflection, I realized that these words were profound symbols of many of my life stories. Yet the stories or symbols did not represent a sequential story, but were more of a montage or mandala of images and events.

For instance, the symbol of "exposed film" brought back my adolescence, which was often fraught with ambiguity. I was so naive and filled with idealism; the light-sensitive grains only needed to be exposed and a myriad of pictures would appear on the blank celluloid of my young life. And so they did—leaving a foundation for young adulthood. As Ann Johnson wrote, "Experiences . . . are often expressed in visceral terms: *gut-wrenching, heart-breaking, mind-bending, side-splitting, stunning*." My adolescent film clearly showed all that and more. But as soon as I recaptured that one story, I realized that my "exposed film" has been part of my twenties, thirties, and forties stories as well as my adolescence. Nothing seemed to dead-end; the symbol just welled up from time to time.

What are the stories that fit the words, symbols, and phrases of the six chapters of your life?

But what does this have to do with maturity? Lately we have all been conditioned to think of life in terms of stages or levels, for example, the patterns of Erikson, Fowler, Gilligan, or Belenky. Yet my ongoing relationships with women (and Ann Johnson's reflections) seem to speak of synchronous development, the spiral enfolding and unfolding, the contiguous integration rather than the rungs of stepladder maturation.

We do not have many Jacob's ladders or Towers of Babel in women's maturation. Instead, just as Mary kept all things in her heart (cf. Lk 2:19), women's maturation seems more like holding and nurturing. It seems like rummaging around the sacred storeroom (cf. Mt 13:52) and knowing when to pull out the diverse contents that it contains. It is finding a treasure in a field (cf. Mt 13:44) that would have been overlooked because you perhaps thought being a woman was not as important as being a man.

What are your favorite scriptural quotes or stories that speak of your maturation as a woman?

Johnson's article also reminded me of Joseph Campbell's work with mythology's patterns. In his cross-cultural book *The Hero with a Thousand Faces,* he speaks of several stages of the heroine's/hero's journey that also resonate with "child, kin, helper, and creator." He claims that every sacred mythic hero or heroine follows a similar journey. You might enjoy plotting your life below with this adaptation of his work:

LEAVING HOME—time when you are forced out and have to fend for yourself:	*When did you leave home or the safe secure womb?*
THE CHALLENGE—what you are alive for, what you need to live for:	*What is your challenge or your risk-taking about?*
NAMING THE DEMONS—knowing how you can get sidetracked in life and how that could dim your vision:	*Name your demons.*
FINDING THE MAGICAL HELPERS—realizing that you are protected and cared for beyond measure:	*Who are your helpers– those who have helped you work with your demons and offer protection?*
SLAYING THE DRAGON—meeting the challenge and living through the ambiguity and danger of leaving home:	*How did you slay your dragon? Or did you make friends with it and now have it as a helper?*
GOING HOME—returning the integrated person who has both the blessing and the tamed/wild dragon within:	*When and how did you return home? How did it feel as you returned?*
GIVING A BLESSING—reaching out and extending the blessing so others can leave home:	*What is your blessing, and to whom will you give it?*

In my work with women in adult education, perhaps the best thing that happens is that they see that they have a lot to offer the world in their maturation. The hidden light under the bushel basket has inexhaustible fuel after the basket is lifted. However, the basket was necessary for most who experienced wombing, tombing, or just plain fear.

Long ago, a male friend said to me about the groups of women with whom I was working: "Do you know what you are doing to those women every time you meet with them? They are laughing and crying, searching for meaning, seeing new visions, muddling through, and arguing. . . ." Yes, he was right. Adult education can be a powerful revelation. It can unearth the polished diamond, dig the tunnel leading to new horizons, or point to the brilliant star set against the darkness.

Describe times when adult education was a powerful revelation for people with whom you worked.

As adult educators, our task is often seen as more directly related to the transmission of content than to the process of maturation. However, in the last few years, I have decided that maturation is primary. I made this choice after seeing that the "way" of adult education was clearly what made the difference for people with whom I worked. If I were a mentor, facilitator, changer-agent, challenger, and risk-taker "with" the people I met, then the child, kin, helper, and creator in them emerged almost immediately. They could tell me the content of the gospel, the meaning of life, the sacredness of their relationships.

I never like separating the human race. In my experience, Ann's words of *child, kin, helper, Creator* are somewhat distinctive for women's maturation, but they do not preclude the experiences of men. Women's ways of maturation cannot be isolated or categorized as completely different from men's, but surely men will recognize that the mature woman has a uniqueness that they would find refreshing to sit with and bask in.

There is a hunger for growing wise, for creating something decent, for justice and peace, for an ecological unity grounding us and lifting us beyond our planet. Satisfying this hunger is no small task. Yet maturation is within our grasp because the child is in the woman (man) as the woman (man) is in the child. The kin is ripe for kithing (the art of spiritual presence), and the helpers have no shortage of mutual tasks. The created is in the Creator as the Creator is in the least speck of creation. Maturation is potent and only needs to be trusted. The Spirit is groaning, as St. Paul says in his letter to the Corinthians, for all to come to fullness. Let it be.

What Prevents Adult Christians from Becoming Mature?

Dennis L. O'Connor

How narrow the gate and constricted the road that leads to life. And those who find it are few (Mt 7:14).

. . . it is the greatest of all disciplines to know oneself; for when a man knows himself, he knows God (Clement of Alexandria, *Paedagogus*).[1]

So be perfect, just as your heavenly Father is perfect (Mt 5:48).

Centuries before the followers of Jesus were called *Christians,* they named themselves *people of the Way.* As pilgrims and sojourners forever incomplete and in process, we carry the cross of our personal and societal brokenness as we inch toward wholeness and peace. St. Augustine expresses our condition when he calls Jesus "our native country" and "the way to that country."[2] From one Christian perspective, then, wholeness and maturity entail a journey of return and discovery, of reconciliation with the living God, who is at once the way, the end, the energy, and guide of wayfarers. But to retrieve our lost identity and recover our full self, we must undergo a healing transformation of consciousness known as *metanoia* or conversion.

To understand what prevents adult Christians from becoming mature, we must move in and out of the paradox that grounds and manifests this maturity. The paradox is God's personal and uncondi-

---

[1] Cited in "The Structure and Dynamics of the Self," *Aion: Researches into the Phenomenology of the Self,* vol. 9, part II, *The Collected Works of Carl G. Jung,* R. F. Hull, trans., Bollingen Series XX (Princeton University Press, 1951), p. 222.

[2] *On Christian Doctrine,* D. W. Robertson, Jr., trans. (Indianapolis, 1958), p. 13; cited in William J. Bouwsma, "Christian Adulthood," *Daedalus* 105 (Spring 1976): 86.

tional love for each of us, which both roots us in reality and calls into question the norms and values of every society.[3]

Our argument has three parts. It begins with Christian maturity's paradoxical identification of child and adult in Jesus. This broken and abandoned one, this abysmal failure by any society's standard of success, nevertheless embodies in his degradation and shame the wholeness we seek. The second part explores obstacles to maturity and resistances to self-knowledge and conversion. Here biblical spirituality illumines the issues through a comparison of Abraham and our first parents and a meditation on the parable of the Prodigal Son. The final section links Christian maturity, self-knowledge, and conversion. Drawing on the Desert Fathers and some Jungian reflections on individuation, I return to the theme of spiritual childhood and consider why few of us choose to undergo conversion and become the good news in our world.

At Once Child and Adult in Christ Jesus

The title of this essay brims with paradox, for Christian adulthood would seem, in one sense, a contradiction in terms. As William J. Bouwsma has shown, normative Christianity recognizes that "the goal of human development is total conformity to the manhood of Christ. But since this is a transcendent goal, the practical emphasis in Christian adulthood is on the process rather than its end."[4] Granted that "the measure of true adulthood is finally the full stature of Christ (Eph 4:13)," Bouwsma argues that this absolute standard means that "no man, whatever his age, can claim to be fully an adult."[5] And because Christianity stresses

[3] Only from within the paradox of unconditional divine love can one renounce society's norms for happiness and success; turn totally to God; embrace failure, poverty, and rejection; become like a little child; and fully trust the Father. But from a perspective *outside* the paradox, the tradition of Western philosophical rationalism, for example, such behavior is irresponsible and immature. Lacking categories to interpret and accept wisdom, it must dismiss Christian belief and teaching as infantile delusion and blatant foolishness. But unlike Western rationalism, the Mahayana Buddhist tradition is at home in the ways of the spirit, including paradox. Being grounded in mystery and silence and in the rigorous pursuit of wholeness through compassionate service and loving detachment, it understands and praises radical simplicity. Thus, we have the Chinese Buddhist proverb: "The mind of a child is the mind of a Buddha."

[4] Bouwsma, "Christian Adulthood," p. 80.

[5] Ibid.

> the capacity for growth [as a constant potential], the Christian life is like adolescence [which, in turn, suggests] the coexistence, within the personality, of the child. . . . Adulthood assumes that the child cannot be left behind, but is the basis of the more mature personality. Thus the child lives on in the man, so that the child and man are somehow identical, a conclusion, from the standpoint of classical manhood, that is paradoxical and absurd.[6]

What, then, is the relationship between maturity and Christ? Jesus is the Perfect Man, the embodiment of wholeness, the archetype of the Self, the fully mature and responsible human being. In the words of Archbishop Anthony Bloom, "he is man as God willed him."[7] To know Jesus is to meet God, in whose presence I see myself as I was meant to be. Our master, ideal, and brother, Jesus is also our physician stretching forth his hand in healing, our lover demolishing every wall of separation within and between us. Daring intimacy with the living God, he embraces a shameful death alone and in torment, becoming one with us through sharing and healing our deepest wounds of inferiority and alienation.

Obstacles to Maturity

What prevents us from becoming mature also keeps us from becoming fully ourselves. As Kierkegaard argued in *The Sickness Unto Death*, despair is refusing to be myself and rejecting the Holy Spirit, the cause of all life, growth, and transformation. From a Christian perspective, immaturity involves refusing to know and accept myself and carry the cross of my unique identity. My refusal to be responsibly present presupposes that where and who I am are insufficient or unacceptable. Thus, I seek distraction, becoming deaf and blind to God's summoning presence. Such fearful distancing and distrust recall the contrast between our first parents and Abraham. After they sin, Adam and Eve hide from God's call to self-knowledge and loving intimacy. No longer simply and wholly present, they are spectators to themselves, fugitives from the depth and beauty of their experience, now ashamed of their own nakedness. God, of course, is that depth manifest in the playful self-giving of responsible sexual love. Since the divine gift of sexuality is our most delicate physical and spiritual dimension, any disruption there may cause self-distancing or evasion.

---

[6] Ibid., p. 81.

[7] Archbishop Anthony Bloom, *Meditations: A Spiritual Journey through the Parables* (Denville, N.J.: Dimension Books, 1971), p. 87.

Estranged from God and their bodies (where else can spiritual intimacy take place?), they become anxiously self-conscious. Abraham, on the other hand, is the ideal person of faith who characteristically responds, "Here I am Lord." His simple answer to God's call, in contrast to Adam and Eve's tortuous disclaimers, illustrates the difference between neurotic complexity and genuine depth.

This refusal to be present informs the parable of the Prodigal Son,[8] which reveals our own variety of spiritual absence and immaturity.

Craving pleasure, autonomy, and boundless freedom, the younger son is not present to himself or to the reality of his father's love. Demanding his share of the inheritance, he, in effect, wants his father dead and gone so that he can live on his own without ties or responsibilities. He presumes, of course, that he will remain forever irresistibly young, healthy, and rich in a world free of God and the grave. And to show who is in charge, he goes off to a distant country. In other words, he has left his native land and fallen into his false self, a state of oblivion and unconsciousness chosen as an alternative to being present and accountable. His outward journey confirms the sundering distance created when he denied his identity as a son and brother. Rootless, blind, and addicted to sensual pleasure, he can delight in nothing else. Bereft and deluded, he is in crisis—in mortal danger—but he does not know that yet.

But is the older son in any better shape? Judgmental, merciless, choking with resentment, he obeys his father's orders but he misses the Order of Love, which is *the whole point* of this life and its only justification. Missing that life-giving love, he also misses himself, his own freedom and goodness: in rigid, self-justifying despair, he fastens on the false identity of the principled slave obeying orders. Surrounded by love—the very Love that moves the entire universe—and invited to share in the mystery of gracious service, he can only imagine grudging servitude, for he, too, has yet to learn what it means to be his father's son. In this paradise of intimacy, he feels unloved and desolate: like ourselves, he has neither the eyes to see nor the ears to hear the good news.

The crushing force of shame and hunger taught the younger brother to recall his identity and return to his father, if only as a servant. But the older son has clearly never been young or lived in his body or risked being imperfect and passionate: he does not know himself and still cannot come to his senses. He, too, has gone off to a distant country and squandered his inheritance, but, in this instance, the foreign country is his own mind that keeps him remote and blind

---

[8] Bloom, Jung, Rilke, and Sanford have influenced my reading of the parable.

to his father's love. Pathetically puffed up with compensatory self-importance, he cannot distinguish between feast or famine or life and death, because it is all the same to him. Shut in upon himself in a weatherless room of abiding anger, he desires a feast but misses the feast within and without. For although he has been given a great deal, his clenched hands have received precious little. He craves triumph and vindication, but his father can only offer the daily bread of love and reconciliation. And so he will remain miserable and heartsick until he stops desiring to prove his father wrong and exalt his puny delusion of how the world should be run.

In several ways, this parable sheds light on our own condition. First, it makes us responsible for maturing and working diligently in the world: no one else can shoulder that burden. The prodigal must return to his father's disciplined love to learn responsibility and joy in contributing to the family's welfare. Second, it communicates the father's respectful love: only their well-being matters; he has no desire to compare, judge, or control. Third, spiritual growth occurs as I let go my illusions and realize that God is truly the Lord of the living and has mastery over every part of my being. I become more awake and present as I put myself at his disposal, accept his will, and do the work I am called to do. For, as one of the Desert Fathers said, "whatever you see your soul desire according to God, do that thing, and you shall keep your heart safe."[9] Fourth, it shows how the brothers' mutual reflection paradoxically bonds and condemns them to becoming one another's shadow self, two sides of one person, unconscious of the other's value. Their distortions of affections, will, and intellect can be healed, that is, made whole and holy, by submitting to their father's ordering love. And fifth, it reveals God's plan for us: a fully conscious and joyful life ("All that I have has always been yours"). We are called to be as creative and passionately accepting as he is: he loves us, *all* of us, not some rarified fraction of ourselves. Unlike the older brother who scrounges to find what he *thinks* is acceptable—legalistic obedience—and then fearfully distorts what he clings to, we know in Christ Jesus that we are called to be whole and complete since every part of us is to be known, reverenced, and integrated. We are not called to extol one part of ourself over the rest, nor are we to deny or junk *any* part of the temple of God that we are.

The parable also shows the paradox of weakness, moral failing, and imperfection in the spiritual life. On the one hand, the cultural juggernaut of family, school, and church—all the agents and custodians

[9] Thomas Merton, trans., *The Wisdom of the Desert: Sayings from the Desert Fathers of the Fourth Century* (New York: New Directions, 1960), p. 26.

of socialization and indoctrination—as well as the monumental authority of Jewish and Christian law, legalism, and morality resoundingly inveigh against every manner of moral failing and imperfection. Yet on the other hand, Luke does not propose a middle way between the brothers, whose respective imperfections seem to represent extremes on a spectrum of spiritual sensibility. Do the varieties of religious experience entail varieties of inescapable human imperfection? Should one aspire to perfection through obedient obliteration of one's own desires and selfless dedication to serving the needs of others? Can one grow in the Lord without the agony of conversion?

Although I cannot answer these questions, experience teaches me that weakness, not strength, is the way to wholeness and intimacy with God. For our weakness irrefutably reveals who and where we are. Our needs—not our achievements (which can blind us to our limitations)—plunge us into crisis, where we must find a way or go under. As the parable suggests, our neediness can make us aware that there *is* a crisis, that we must *act*, that we can *choose* to trust God. The younger brother's hunger and desolation lead him to confess humbly his weaknesses and sins, acknowledge his present degradation, and struggle to return to his father. Having done so, he is paradoxically already home safe in his father's love long before his father comes into view.

Wisdom is also at work in the older brother's weakness. Outraged by his father's apparent moral collapse into mindless glee when the younger son turns up, he bars his heart as never before, pouring forth years of suppressed anger and hurt and frustrated love. Sometimes the desire for control leads us to deny our feelings and strangle our honest cries for help. But now that the older brother has exploded the self-protective myth of the dutiful son, he has the chance to deal honestly with his father and face his own need for love and reconciliation.

Many things can prevent us from becoming mature and blind us to the beauty, dignity, and goodness of the transcendent God radiantly alive in us. "Were not our hearts burning within us?" said the disciples one to another after the great epiphany at Emmaus. Feeling the Lord's saving presence irradiating them with joy and hope, they were jolted awake as though for the first time, suddenly ready to race home with the good news. In fact, they *became* the good news, just as the prodigal son's change of heart and humble confession was his father's good news and his own new life. What prevents *us,* then, from being the good news in our own world? For I assume this is part of Christian maturity.

What prevents us from desiring wholeness and seeking the face of the living God? Jesus's invitation, ". . . be perfect, just as your heavenly Father is perfect," summons us to *completion and not to some platonic ideal of disembodied moral flawlessness*. Yet too often we get the message in our early years that our goodness, our value, resides in our being *good*. But, surely, if goodness is to mature and we are to go beyond dutifully avoiding mud puddles, we must risk learning about ourselves and our world through exploration and experiment. This inevitably means learning through trial and errors galore.

Without such learning, our problem solving will remain critically barren, for we would never have acted and suffered defeat. Instead, we would have been spectators with little chance to learn why Jesus had to give his life for us, why human life is infinitely valuable (that is, worth the life of God). Indeed, unless we have made and learned from bushels of mistakes as we strive toward individuation, how could we ever discover our own hunger and thirst, our truly insatiable need for communion with the living God?

The human challenges facing us are more on the order of the Pacific Ocean than they are of that tempting mud puddle by the white picket fence. Grave problems in ecology, health, nutrition, peace and social justice, political stability, education, economic well-being, employment, family welfare, equal opportunity, human development, and quality of work-life confront us at the global, national, regional, and local levels. Their very magnitude and complexity suggest our need for deeply educated and committed minds and hearts eager to seek the face of God in every dimension of human service.

If we are to become mature, self-differentiated, and perfect in the gospel sense of complete and fulfilled in our experience, then we should consider the role of the family, schools, and churches in this regard. I spoke earlier of the need to make mistakes galore (think of how a child learns to walk or skate). Most schools, I suspect, ignore that model of human learning. Like the typical workplace, they are interested in results (read *success*), not mistakes. Moreover, flexibility, imagination, and free experimentation are not values likely to be championed in many homes and certainly not in schools where control, socialization, and indoctrination are the norm.

And since the churches necessarily reflect the strengths and weaknesses of their peculiar history and culture, we often find an emphasis upon conformity, orthodoxy, and obedience. This emphasis can alienate people, discourage their creativity, and distance them from the transcendent by convincing them that their religious experience has nothing to offer.

Surely, we need to find ways to nurture this spiritual growth and to encourage creativity and individuation. Otherwise, we will stand guilty of the charge Jung levelled in 1939, when he said that Christianity often distorts Jesus' teaching so that "the faithful *remain* children instead of becoming *as* children, and they do not gain their life because they have not lost it."[10] The choice, as Jung sees it—and I would agree—is between fundamentally different attitudes that promote, in his judgment, either infantilism or maturity.

When Jesus spoke of emulating little children, he was not encouraging childishness or immaturity. Rather, he paradoxically urges us to become mature by imitating their sense of wonder and delight, their fresh spontaneity and openness, their readiness to believe the best and to trust those who love them, for children can be simple, direct, and in touch with their unconscious, the source of all creativity. He enjoins us, then, to abandon pretense and duplicity, speak only from the heart, cry out *and expect* God's help in our every need, and believe that his love will make us whole. This will seem foolish according to the norms and games of our culture, especially when one is spontaneous rather than calculating; simple and straightforward rather than devious and secretive; and free from cynicism, despair, judgmentalism, and the needing to be first. Intimate communion with the Spirit allows the mature Christian to travel lightly without elaborate strategies, defenses, or systems. Free from such anxiety, one may rest in Isaiah's wisdom: "By waiting and by calm you shall be saved, in quiet and in trust your strength lies" (30:15). Full consciousness and complete presence are, in this order, perfectly in keeping with childlike trust.

Christian Maturity, Self-Knowledge, and Conversion

Maturing in the Lord is a strenuously interactive process. It is not an abstract noun whose static meaning we coolly master before graduating to the mysteries of divine syntax. There *is* nothing to learn beyond God; indeed, the only learning that can take place *in* God is revelation, the silent probing and sifting that inexorably call our very life into question. The God who thus reveals himself as he addresses us is that narrow gate and the constricted road that lead to life. This narrowness, like the birth canal itself, makes us squeeze through in anguish one at a time, as individuals, not as part of a tribe or class, let alone as club members banking on privilege and preferential treatment. It permanently dims the bright world of cultural assurances, dissolving the plastic identities and certainties conferred by circumstance, wealth, place, and title. Naked we came into the world and

---

[10] "The Difference Between Eastern and Western Thinking," Part I of *Psychological Commentary on the "Tibetan Book of the Great Liberation"; Psychology and Religion: West and East*, vol. 11; *The Collected Works of Carl G. Jung*, R. F. Hull, trans., Bollingen Series XX (Princeton: Princeton University Press, 1958), cited in Joseph Campbell, ed., *The Portable Jung* (New York: Viking Penguin, 1971), p. 483.

naked do we come into the One whose holiness consumes everything that is not real and true. Stripped of artifice, defenses, and all the alternatives to simple intimacy, I face the cleansing truth that I am ever a child and only a beginner.

Self-knowledge requires *individuation*, a slow process of self-discovery and separation from collective thinking and attendant judgmentalism. Perfect love, as St. Paul teaches, casts out fear, which rules where love and self-knowledge are absent. Learning to love and honor myself and my neighbor, I relinquish the fear and hatred that characterize racism, classism, sexism, parochialism, homophobia, clericalism, and all the other refusals to honor the living God present in every person. In giving up authoritarianism for authentic ministry, I move away from patriarchal modes and norms to explore responsible community in light of absolute human equality, where all our many gifts may flourish, intimacy and service are valued, and self-differentiation is encouraged.

The varieties of fear and distrust of human equality suggest the extent of our own unconsciousness, immaturity, and resistance. This lack of personal and social consciousness also affects those institutions that build and sustain our culture. For better or worse, they provide—or fail to provide—the models, structures, mores, rationales, and rewards for building a mature identity. Thus, to some degree and in various ways, the institutions of family, church, and school participate in and strengthen this cultural unconsciousness and resistance to individuation.

Such resistance makes individuation unthinkable to many who, as John Sanford explains,

> . . . hate and fear individuality, with its demands for freedom and consciousness, and so reject the kingdom of God. In so doing, they reject the inner world, whose recognition destroys that identification with a group that shields us from the demands of becoming an individual.[11]

Narrowness suggests pain and danger as well as the trauma of being born: we speak of "narrow escape," "tight spot," "shrinking in terror." No wonder *narrow* is the root meaning of anxiety or dread in English and a dozen other languages. Anxiously sensing that I am all alone, I struggle to imagine and find the gate (no easy task in this century) and make it through as best I can. No one can be conscious for

---

[11] *The Kingdom Within: The Inner Meaning of Jesus' Sayings*, rev. ed. (San Francisco: Harper and Row, 1987), p. 45.

me; just as no one can love or die or be born for me. The task of self-knowledge remains personal and obdurately simple: as Mohandas Gandhi analogously observed, "there is no road to peace; there is only peace."

Why does Jesus say that only a few find it? From a psychological perspective, maturation entails integrating every part of the self. The injunction, "Take up your cross daily and come follow me," means to bear the burden of the full self, with all its conflicts and tensions. Spiritually, it implies Christian conversion, which is hardly natural or pleasant. Only a rare person would choose full consciousness, thus crucifying the ego's illusions and delusions, while facing and integrating disturbing parts of the self that the ego rejects, and nurturing and honoring them as they deserve. Perhaps Christ's descent into hell and resurrection from the dead suggest a corollary to this spiritual death and rebirth of the self.

Conversion may involve far more than we can either understand or consent to rationally. As the supreme threat to the ego, it demands the whole of who I am—my past, present, and future; my conscious and unconscious; my power to name myself, try to control my destiny, and judge the quality of my life.

In this connection, I remember Anthony de Mello's stunning answer to the question, Why is God invisible? "He isn't." Yet just as we never see the screen because we are absorbed by the film projected on it, so too, de Mellow insists, we keep projecting ourselves on to God and never see him. To know God and ourselves, we must own and withdraw these projections and begin *doing* "the will of my Father in heaven" (Mt 7:21). Anything less would seem self-delusory.

Our persistent blindness is a recurring theme in the no-nonsense sayings of the Desert Fathers:

> The reason why we do not get anywhere is that we do not know our limits, and we are not patient in carrying on the work we have begun. But without any labor at all we want to gain possession of virtue.[12]

Conversion, then, is often a surprisingly slow and painful process. But the men and women who persevered understood that changing one's heart can take a lifetime. Thus, Abbot Ammonas spent fourteen years praying day and night to be delivered from anger.[13] Imagine how long it might take to stop judging others and to hate evil as Abbot Poeman

---

12. Merton, *The Wisdom of the Desert*, p. 34.

13. Cf. ibid., p. 33.

tells us: "that man hates evil who hates his own sins, and looks upon every brother as a saint, and loves him as a saint."[14]

Maturity is the fruit of conversion that brings us into the presence of God. Through conversion, we choose to become responsible for our life, receiving it as a gift given in trust. Now that we know we belong to God, our existence is not random or absurd, our identity not of our own creation but rooted in the intimate life of the Trinity, the pattern and fulfillment of all intimacy. Awakened, I begin to see myself honestly in God within the context of the world, my family, and society, and all the relationships and responsibilities that entails.

To see myself with such honesty is to come naked and unaccommodated—the only way possible—into God's presence. In doing so, I drop every label, credential presumption, and excuse; acknowledge the willfulness that delays or dilutes this encounter; and realize I am always and only a beginner. As Thomas Merton noted in moving to his hermitage at Gethsemene, "None of us likes to be a beginner. But in the spiritual life that's all we ever are"—even Merton.

---

[14] Ibid., p. 71.

Aiding the Conversion Process
A Challenge for Adult Educators

Edmund F. Gordon

I would like to begin this reflection by sharing three experiences. Not long ago, I was preparing an adult education program on "A Spirituality for Mid-Life." As part of the preparation, I gathered a group of middle-aged men from a local parish, most of whom were professionals or owners of their own small businesses. The purpose of the session was to obtain their reactions to the program's topics and themes. During the session, I mentioned that one of the topics to be covered was the mid-life crisis. To my surprise, the men reacted very negatively. "Hey," one of them said, "we are successful problem-solvers and managers. We are trained to avoid crises; but when they happen, we deal with them. We manage." Several other members of the group agreed.

Another time I heard a bishop, who was about to address a group on the topic of evangelization, say, "How do you talk about evangelization and conversion with people who are so comfortable?" He did not have an answer that night, and I do not know if he has one yet.

The third experience comes from reading Dennis O'Connor's article. Perhaps it was the topic, or maybe it was the style, but for some reason, I ended up experiencing O'Connor more keenly than his message. He came through his words as an intense believer, an avid searcher of deeper religious meaning.

All three of these experiences have influenced my reflections on adult religious education. The first two have helped me curb the temptation to assume that parishes are filled with people who see religious maturity as linked to a conversion process. The third experience has caused me to ponder the approaches we should take to promote better ongoing conversion within adult religious education.

If my first two experiences reflect common attitudes in our parishes, and I believe that they do, particularly in white and/or middle-class ones, then an approach to adult religious education that orientates learners toward maturity and therefore toward conversion will not be an easy task. In fact, I am not sure we have really examined our programs in light of these factors.

I would like to begin, then, by reflecting on some of the characteristics of adult religious education that promote or assist the process of conversion, keeping in mind O'Connor's comments that the process "can take a lifetime" and is often "surprisingly slow and painful."

1. Adult religious education for conversion has to accept people where they are.

Any religious educator I know would be ecstatic to have a parish filled with O'Connors, with intense searchers and questioners. But the reality seems to be that there are many more persons like the members of my focus group or the bishop's audience: good willed, but comfortable with a static faith. If these persons are to move beyond where they are, it will not be because I or any other person tells them they should be someplace else. Indeed, they will become very defensive—and rightly so—if they feel that they are somehow seen to be not as "faithful" as the more searching, questioning type of believers.

Too often, we adult religious educators fail to remember that our people are at very different places on the path of faith and that their needs and their perceptions of their needs are very diverse. So, in designing our adult programs, we need to find ways both to rouse those who are too comfortable in their faith and to satisfy those who seriously quest for spiritual growth.

2. Adult religious education for conversion needs to embody the skills of critical reflection.

O'Connor realizes that the path to maturity includes a process of self-discovery, of separation from "collective thinking and attendant judgmentalism." It appears to me that the skill of critical reflection is an essential tool for one who wants to move along the path of self-discovery and conversion. However, until recently we have not considered the teaching of that skill to be central to our ministry.

The methodologies of Thomas Groome, Paulo Friere, and others that embody critical reflection have helped us to shift the goals of adult religious education from information transferral to human transformation and conversion.

I can still remember the first time that I added the following questions to a learning process: "Why do you do what you do?" and "What will happen if you keep doing what you do?" They changed the dynamics of the entire event.

3. Adult education for conversion and maturity must always link faith and life.

O'Connor's comments are predicated on the basic insight that our lives and our faith must be one if we are to attain Christian maturity. Remember my focus group, however. Those men did not feel any need for a conversion. They felt fine about things. They had life pretty much under control. They were managers! And there are many men and women of all ages who are similar to them. Indeed, they might even comprise the majority in our parishes.

When I have probed beyond the surface with persons of this type, I have often found that they have compartmentalized their lives in terms of faith and life. They live a faith that allows two identities, two worlds to live in, to worship in. They do not see the connections or the contradictions. While many of them can talk about and document the course of their careers and their financial and professional growth, they are stymied when asked to speak about the growth of their spiritual lives. They often have great ambitions in this life but small ambitions regarding their relationship with God (except, of course, at the end of the line).

We need to take more time to develop adult education processes that will help such people break down the barriers between their two worlds. Linking faith and life is not a new item on the adult education agenda. Yet, I think it is still more talked about than practiced. For example, where parishes have moved beyond offering theology-type programs, they have often replaced them with secular-oriented programs with prayer attached. While there is nothing wrong with either a theology program or a secular program, I do not think either will really do the trick. What we need is to integrate them.

As an example, suppose we offered a program on "Aging Parents." Besides helping the participants to come to terms with how they can best assist their parents and to cope with some of the pressures of the "sandwiched generation," an integrated program would help them reflect on what the Scriptures have to say about aging and parents, would help them to reflect on moral decision making, and would help them learn to pray through the difficult times.

It is a real challenge to develop programs of this nature because they demand a lot more thought than programs where we first bring in the nursing-home specialist, then the gerontologist, and finally, on the last week, the chaplain.

4. Adult education for conversion and maturity must address the heart as well as the head.

O'Connor uses emotionally laden words such as *passion* and *passionately* throughout the article. In fact, the language of the entire article bespeaks a man who, like Jacob, is deeply involved in the struggle with the angel. Growth comes with the struggle.

I have heard many adult religious educators speak with frustration (and a little envy) about the large turnouts for any program that has to do with Medjugorje while they have only a few individuals at their programs on, say, social justice. Too often, we forget that conversion involves a "change of heart." This is not to deny that one can have an intellectual conversion or that the mind is an important part of the human person. However, the mind is not the whole person, nor is it the locus of the passion, the terror, or the existential need that O'Connor so eloquently expresses in his article.

To that end, it might be good to remember the works of one of the early modern English catechists, Francis Drinkwater, who was concerned that religious education find a language that would be able to speak to the heart. He described four language types that are used in religious education. The first two he labeled *scientific-difficult* and *scientific-simple*. The former is the technical language of theology, with its own vocabulary, and so forth. The latter includes the language of the catechism or of the "technical manual" for nontechnicians. (I always think of the many confusing owner's manuals that come with electronic and computer hardware.) Drinkwater did not find either of these types to be "user friendly."

The other two types he labeled *poetic-difficult* and *poetic-simple*. Poetic-difficult is the language of the more obscure poets, the ones you have to read several times to grasp their meaning. The final style, poetic-simple, included for Drinkwater, the Scriptures, especially the psalms and parables. They have a language that is easily understood and touches the heart as well as the mind.

In our time, those individuals who have begun to explore story forms and narrative theology may be closest in thinking to this English catechist. Stories seem to carry many levels of feeling and thought and have a power to engage the whole person.

Of course there is always a danger that once one moves into the arena of feeling and emotion, manipulation is more possible. Our experience of many televangelists leaves us no doubt that emotionalism is not the way to go. On the other hand, an anemic, antiseptic head-trip may have little appeal to the average person in the pew.

Raymond Nogar, a Dominican philosopher and theologian, once wrote:

> In short, we do not need a demonstration of God's existence today; we need a demonstration of His personal presence among us. Christ did not come to demonstrate His Father's existence, but to witness to His presence among us. . . . We don't need a God we can admire; we need a God we can believe in, one in whom we can place our trust and love. We need to recognize God personally present to us in our day, personally speaking to us. There is only one sign of personal, loving presence, and though it may be hard to define or even describe, no one misses it.[1]

[1] Raymond J. Nogar, OP, *The Lord of the Absurd* (New York: Herder and Herder, 1966), p. 138.

That is what is missing from too much of our adult religious education.

5. Adult religious education for maturity and conversion needs to be about spiritual direction.

Over the last few years, I have become increasingly convinced that the missing link in most of our catechumenal processes is *spiritual direction.* If we saw more of the process as spiritual direction, we might not be so tempted to turn the catechumenate into a mini theology course or to be so concerned about the content of each session. Likewise, the kind of spiritual maturity that O'Connor describes is usually achieved under the direction of a "spiritual master," and not as the result of a theology course (though no one can control the Spirit).

Throughout his article, O'Connor speaks of the need for individuation as a key ingredient in maturity. It is precisely because we are individuals who move at different paces along the path of faith that an individual spiritual director is essential for anyone who takes the journey seriously. I think we have begun to improve in this area, but much greater energy has to be expanded to meet the needs of the searchers in the community. Too often, we see them leave the community because they see no way to fit in.

6. Adult religious education for maturity and conversion needs to live with paradox and tension.

In many ways, this characteristic is related to the one above. O'Connor is convinced that maturation calls for the individual to stand alone before God, to individuate, to separate oneself from harmful collectivism. He also seems to suggest that churches and other well-intentioned organizations can keep people from maturing rather than help them grow. Is this a fair critique of much of adult religious education? What do we intend for the individuals who participate in our programs and processes? Can we present programs that promote maximum freedom while showing that the same freedom is expressed within a community? Can we find ways to promote the individual without destroying the community or to promote the community without destroying the individual?

Can adult religious education find ways to assist people to deal with the paradoxes of faith so well expressed by O'Connor? Here, it might be good to keep in mind that the degree of faith development expressed by the author would, I believe, be "Level 5" in the topology of James Fowler. In his studies, Fowler has not found many individuals who reach this stage much before mid-life. Perhaps, as the baby-boom generation begins to move through mid-life, there might be more openness to explore the paradoxes of life and faith. If so, the difficulty would be to resist the temptation to come up with some simplistic answers to difficult questions.

There are some who believe that the *Universal Catechism*, when it is published, will solve many of the problems of the contemporary Church. They anticipate that it will provide the tool we need for adult education and, derivatively, for children, to rid us of paradox and tension, to present the faith clearly and unambiguously. O'Connor's article suggests, however, that the essential task of Christian maturation has less to do with a compendium of belief statements then it does with our relationship with God. Again, the words of the wise Dominican, Raymond Nogar, are as true today as when he wrote them for the last generation:

> He cannot be the God of organization, of chancery decrees and monitums issued from distant places, of manuals and rules, some kind of great scoutmaster. He must be dramatically present among us, now. Here is the requirement of belief today: God must come among us and live with us and speak to us today. He must be personally present. That our days are filled with chaos and not celestial harmony is the condition. Let Him come and share this existence with me. It is not "pie in the sky" that I need, not another myth of the eternal return. I need a Lord of my history, a Lord of my todays and tomorrows. Then can I love and trust. Then can I believe.[2]

Can adult religious education help bring this about?

---

[2] Ibid., pp. 140-141.

Christian Maturation
The Later Years

Janice Brewi, CSJ, S.T.D.
Anne Brennan, CSJ, S.T.D.

New Phenomenon

At the turn of the century, the later years for most people were their forties. Life expectancy was forty-seven to forty-nine years. Today, people in the developed world can expect to live well into their eighties.

A century ago, most women died shortly after their child-bearing years. And because men generally died in their forties, there was no great dilemma about life after retirement. So, today's expectation of a longer life for women and men brings the added pressure of both providing financial independence for a "second lifetime" and discerning the moral and spiritual meaning of this second half of life.

Carl G. Jung, writing on the life cycle, said, "A human being would certainly not grow to be seventy or eighty years old if this longevity had no meaning for the species to which he [or she] belongs."[1] Since Jung wrote that over fifty years ago, we have not, as a nation, addressed this meaning. Thus, we have not been able to harness the power and wisdom of our oldest citizens; nor have we been able to support and celebrate their "coming of age."

Certainly, the Church respects all of life's stages. Nevertheless, its institutions need to change more dramatically if they are both to minister to the growing numbers of seniors and to harness their spiritual energies for the sake of others. Vatican II's challenge to respond to the needs of the times has not yet led the Church to study adequately the second half of life and to develop the structures that are needed to address it.

The Life Cycle

We cannot think of "later years" or "old age" without thinking of the life cycle. Old age and its maturation is a fulfillment of the life cycle. We live our life in four primary stages or seasons: childhood, youth, mid-life, and old age or the mature years. Each stage has has its own growth tasks, its own meaning, its own joys and sorrows.

---

[1] Jung. C.G. *Modern Man in Search of a Soul*, W.S. Dell and Cary F. Baynes, trans. (New York: Harcourt, Brace and World, 1933), p. 109.

The Church needs to celebrate the ongoing creation of the human person in all of life's stages. Each Christian must learn to tune in to the making of himself or herself that God is doing in each moment and stage of life. God calls us to enter creatively, cooperatively, and joyfully into the ongoing process of our own personal creation. The ongoing creation, conversion, salvation of each person in all of life's stages has a direct relationship to the health and vitality of the living Body of Christ, the Church, and to the quality of its preaching, community and service.

To understand the final stage of life, a distinction between the first half of life (childhood and young adulthood) and the second half of life (mid-life and mature years) is most helpful.[2] Our culture is youth-oriented and centers on the meaning, tasks, and goals of the first half of life. Twenty or so years of school occupy a good part of the first half of life. During this time, we are not only educated but we also make choices about careers, professions, life commitments, life-styles, and relationships. If marriage and raising a family are to be part of one's life, they, too, are usually accomplished here.

What, then, is the purpose of life's second half? Is it to be only a sad appendage of the first half of life? At one of our Mid-Life Directions Workshops, a woman in her forties said: "I said to my husband on the way here, 'What good can we expect from this workshop? After all, our life together in these twenty-five years has been so good that anything good that happens to us after this will just be icing on the cake.'" Her shortsightedness was verbalizing the culture's expectations. What she was really saying was, "We have done all the real living in these years. We have done all the important, worthwhile, big things; all we can anticipate from life now is 'icing on the cake.'"

Perhaps expecting "only icing" reflects our psyche's expectation of death after forty because for most of human history before *this* century most people did die by forty or shortly after. Our psyche has its remnants of the past just like our bodies do.

At around forty, our youth comes to an end, and with it, our culture's scripts for us. This is a time of both crisis and potential. The person on the threshold of mid-life has reached the fulfillment of youth and is on the brink of a whole new life. Will he or she accept that invitation?

Jung sees life's second half as an opportunity for individuation. This is an opportunity to become more the unique personality we are called to be. Having accomplished the tasks of the first half of life, we can now develop an inner and outer life that fosters personal growth and helps us make a unique contribution to both the care of others and the culture.

---

[2] Cf. ibid., pp. 95-114.

This model of the life cycle sees the ongoing development of the person primarily through the influence of the outer environment as characteristic of the first half of life. The great transition of mid-life is the movement away from the outer environment's being the primary influence on growth to the individual's own inner environment becoming the primary influence. As we enter life's second half, we are called to a greater consciousness of what it is that we have been about in life.

The tasks of the first half of life are, on the whole, more external: education, socialization, finding a niche in society, fitting in, developing skills, working at personal relationships and careers. Although these needs never cease, by mid-life there arises from within a need to know ourselves at a deeper level and to integrate this inner life with our life-style. To become familiar with our inner life and to acquire skills in developing that life is preparing for life's second journey. Becoming comfortable with our inner life enables us to make the changes throughout the second half of life that flow from deep within our personality. This centeredness allows us to live fully the decades ahead rather than to suffer merely the events of aging.

The development of the full personality, the flowering of the Image of God that is uniquely each of us, will be the spiritual journey of life's second half. Interiority developed at this time anchors us in a sense of self and in a sense of the holy deep within ourselves—indeed, in all people and in creation.

By mid-life, we have come to the end of naivete. No longer "innocent," "omnipotent," and "eternal," we have come face to face with limitation, diminishment, and mortality. We have experienced the evil of the world within us and around us. We have sinned and been sinned against and betrayed. We have been around. We have "seen it all," "done it all," and "heard it all."

Reminding us that the first half of life is over are the mirror, the body's ailments and loss of energy, parenting tasks completed, threats of replacement at work, and the deaths of one after another of a whole older generation. Little by little, from these subtle and not so subtle messages of body, calendar, and young people, we know that we are in the second half of life.

As part of, and often as catalyst for, the transition between the first and second halves of life, there arises in many of us a crisis of negative feelings. We go through a period of deadness: feeling monotony, apathy, boredom, indifference, impotence, acedia, suspension in air, a loss of enthusiasm for what was once important and energizing. We can also feel doubt and anxiety, restlessness, a sense of being trapped and desperate, and above all, regret and anger at ourselves and others for choices made or not made.

Without an inner life and centeredness, it is all too easy to identify with these negative feelings over many years. To succumb to them is to become jaded, cynical, and bitter. It is to lose faith in life, hope in life, and love for life.

A New Challenge

The challenge for the Church is to cultivate in the young both healthy inner and outer lives so that when life's second half calls them to a greater inner life, they understand what that means.

Communities will be as strong as the individuals who comprise them. The mature, independent person is one who has the psychic power to enter into community. To discourage the development of individual gifts and talents, vocations, decision making, and discernment is to foster immature, shallow, dependent, compulsive, and addicted personalities and, eventually, to have isolated, stagnant, despairing elders.

A deep, personal inner life in life's second half will root the individual in humanity's spiritual quest. The very survival of the human race may depend on the ability of people in life's second half to meet this challenge and to become the light and salt of the earth.

The Church must now, more than ever, acquaint people with structures for meditation, the art of contemplation, the inner life, and an exultation of the "divine indwelling." At mid-life, when the aging process begins to make itself known in a dramatic way, people are challenged to take precautions and make time for the development of a healthy self-knowledge and a restructuring of their life-style to allow for taking more seriously the word of Jesus, ". . . the kingdom of God is among [within] you" (Lk 17:21). Centered through faith, hope, and love in the God within, the emotional upheavals and disillusionment of a mid-life crisis can become the raw material for creativity and new life.

Owning One's Salvation History

Again and again, throughout the second half of life, we need to ask the existential and spiritual questions: "What really has been going on in the years I have already lived? What has been happening to me?" The Judeo-Christian tradition is steeped in religious story, the story of salvation history. Our Scriptures are filled with the inspired, sacred myths and rituals of a people who knew their life as pilgrimage. Throughout the second half of life, we Christians need to be in touch with our own pilgrimage. The life cycle is a living pilgrimage.

Christians who have celebrated the liturgical year for a lifetime are not strangers to the mysteries of the life of Christ and to how they are appropriated in different ways throughout the life cycle. So too, we come to know and interpret the joyful, glorious, and sorrowful mysteries of our own life journey. Coming to know them at a deeper level, and seeing how we lived through these building moments of our lives helps us understand how they have made us who we are today. We sense the self we were, are, and will still be, coming in and through the elements of our personal history and life story.

To know our story, own our story, appropriate our story, forgive our story, proclaim and celebrate our story is to be on a spiritual journey that continues our story throughout our later years. There can be no Christian maturity in the later years without this. We must be able to discern the good news of our own personal history, to forgive and be healed of its sorrowful events if we are to grow in wisdom and full maturity. This is no easy task and it is one that is never completed.

The joyful, sorrowful, and glorious mysteries of our lives are just that, mysteries. We can never fully understand them. But being in touch with them also puts us in touch with the present mysteries and releases us from fears of future mysteries. We are awakened to the spiritual journey that is life's gift and to the full maturity to which that journey invites us.

We are historical people. We return to our family roots as we explore the history of our ancestors. This is the story of creation and salvation. When, in the last stage of life, we are rooted in this kind of reflection on and celebration of our own salvation history, we have the the basic stuff of maturity—life's wisdom that comes from living an examined life story. We have the basic stuff needed to live the last part of the story with vitality, peace, enthusiasm, and wisdom. We can be guides to others on life's journey.

Knowing our story is never fully complete until we tell our story. Whether it is to a counselor or spiritual director, or to a confidant or friend, we need at times to tell our story. The Stranger on the road to Emmaus asks the two disciples to tell him the story of what happened (cf. Lk 24:19). And it was in the telling of that story that the disciples came to know it in a whole new way. They came to understand the death of Jesus, not as an end, but as a beginning. Their present and future story changed because they came to know their past story at a deeper level.

In the later years of our lives, we must also periodically talk with Christ on our journey. As he did with the disciples on the road to Emmaus, he encourages us also to tell our story. In turn, we ask Christ to "... [s]tay with us, for it is nearly evening and the day is almost over" (Lk 24:29). This is an invitation to have the Lord know our story in a most intimate way, to break bread with us.

Awakening to the sense of the holy in our own story and to the pilgrimage that we are on, to know that there is Someone who knows our story and is with us and leading us on our journey is to be genuinely religious.

> Among all my patients in the second half of life—that is to say, over thirty-five—there has not been one whose problem in the last resort was not that of finding a religious outlook on life. It is safe to say that every one of them fell ill because he [she] had lost that which the living religions of every age have given to their followers, and none of them had really been healed who did not regain his [her] religious outlook.[3]

Losing One's Life to Save It

The mid-life change of life is about psychic change. In childhood and youth, one grows in consciousness and discovers a lot about oneself in the development of the ego. I am a man, a woman, a believer, a nonbeliever, a doctor, lawyer, janitor, scientist, cook. Roles, relationships, qualities, talents, virtues, and vices form our conscious personality or ego.

At mid-life, the psychic orientation moves gradually away from the ego identity of the first half of life to the greater identity of the self. I am more than my ego. My ego is only a part of who I am. I have within my psychic, spiritual self a dormant part, not yet discovered or tapped, the source of new growth and dynamism. I also have within me a part that has been active, though unknown to me. I have ways of being and relating that come from both my own unconscious personal story and from the larger history of the human race that is my inheritance. This unconscious story, personal and collective, is operative, and my new call to greater self-knowledge and individuation demands that I grow conscious of it. Maturation at this crucial point in life allows the driving force of my life to move from the ego to the greater self. Without this shift in consciousness, there can be no maturation.

When this shift begins in mid-life, the mature years reap the fruit. Mid-life is like a death. With this shift, we die to our youth and experience a new birth, the greater self. We lose ourselves to find ourselves. Having experienced the death of the ego as the reigning power, we are prepared for final death and birth into new and eternal life.

The experience of the death of people who have shared intimately our lives is no small matter. Dr. Kübler-Ross gives us the stages of death and dying: denial, bargaining, anger, depression, and creative acceptance. We go through this grieving process again and again. In the midst of this, how does the person in the later years acquire both

---

[3] Ibid., p. 229.

a joyful enthusiasm for life and a peaceful resignation and abandonment in the face of approaching death? The living relationship between ego and self provides the needed vitality as well as the creative acceptance. *In Journal of a Soul*, Pope John XXIII said, "Three-quarters of my contemporaries have passed over to the far shore. So too I must always be ready for the great moment. The thought of death does not alarm me."[4] Even while this statement reflected a genuine part of his mentality and spirituality in his later years, he also remained active and concerned. Indeed, in those same years, he became the profound mover of the Church, affecting a change in its consciousness that was centuries old.

From Unconsciousness to Consciousness

Each infant, while awesome in the fineness and intricacy of its tiny parts, starts life in a state of unconsciousness. Yet, the human child has the inbuilt potential, as no other species has, to come to consciousness. To every child, there comes the momentous day when the light begins to dawn: *This is world and this is I.* The child knows subject from object, and begins to name the world out there. By two years, the child begins to say its insistent "mes" and "nos," as first declaration of separateness, of independence.

As we sacrifice for our values and remain loyal to our commitments in the first half of life, our ego consciousness grows along with our willpower. In trying to live a good Christian life, we struggle to overcome laziness, try to love, are able to stick to something and to work hard. By mid-life, if our ego development has been relatively good, we have put ourselves and something "out there" together, no matter how successful or unsuccessful we (or others) judge ourselves to be. Yet, when we have finally reached this pinnacle, when we seem to know so much about ourselves and our own turf, we begin to feel the earth shake beneath us, as the greater self begins to usurp the ego and take the lead. We may feel that we arrived at the top of the ladder only to discover that it is against the wrong roof. We may feel that we never knew ourselves at all.

In the second half of life, we begin to experience personality change: we have new desires and insights; we feel about things differently. Beginning in mid-life, and continuing throughout the second half of life, there can be the onslaught of experiences that seem like a different or shadow personality. Many a person in the midst of such an experience comes to believe that life to this point has been a complete lie.

---

[4] John XXIII, *Journal of a Soul*, Dorothy White, trans. (New York: McGraw-Hill, 1965), p. 291.

I never really loved you. Our marriage has been a lie. All these years I've been deceiving myself. I married you to get away from home. I finally know what I really want and you're not part of it.

My whole life has been a facade. I became a lawyer (plumber, nurse, teacher, etc.) to please my parents. I'm sick to death of it. I've decided not to tolerate it another day.

I always thought I was faithful (honest, truthful, a believer, a churchgoer, a pacifist, etc.) but now I know it's all been a lie. I've just discovered who I really am. No more hypocrisy for me.

I have sinned in betraying innocent blood. . . . Flinging the money into the temple, he [Judas] departed and went off and hanged himself (Mt 27:4-5).

It is possible to begin to identify with these strong new feelings and to throw over everything that has been built up for forty, fifty, or seventy years.

Fortunately, we do not often transform such statements into action and a whole new reality. They do not usher in collapse but, rather, are the screams of pain at our dawning consciousness that, we are not what we thought ourselves to be. Yes, there has been some lie in our choices, some hate in our loves, some value in what we should not have valued. But, these feelings express a pain that can, in the end, move us, not to destruction, but to needed conversion.

Perhaps our self-image and our living of a relationship, profession, vocation, or faith is too narrow and no longer adequate for whom we need to become. Deep adjustments, new places in which to put energy, new causes, and greater love may be what the Spirit is initiating with our growing dissatisfaction, disillusionment, or discontentment.

To totally repress one's former self and one's former life is a great catastrophe that can, and does, happen to people in the second half of life. Yet, there is another catastrophe just as terrible. It is to close off growth, to die at fifty and not be buried until ninety. That happens when we deny, ignore, suppress, and repress every new desire, insight, doubt, question, dissatisfaction, invitation, dream, or experience that we have. It is to proclaim over and over through the fifties, sixties, eighties, or nineties, "I never did (said, thought, felt, imagined, asked) that before, and I am certainly not going to start now."

To totally collapse every value, truth, love, or commitment of the first half of life is certainly not Christian maturity, but neither is it to see ourselves finished at fifty or seventy-five. Neither is it to become closed and rigid or to build walls around values, attitudes, and habits of the first half of life. Nor is it to be self-righteous and intolerant of others and of our own inner movements. This is stagnation, not integrity. Rather, Christian maturity calls for us to stand outside of roles, habits, taboos, attitudes, patterns of perception, and judgements. We need to loosen the hold on our compulsiveness.

So many of our habits and taboos in later years are remnants of the "no-nos" of an enculturated, biased childhood and youth. As we adapted to the world in the first half of life, the more something about us was unacceptable to a parent or to some other important group, or to a role we chose, the more it had to be repressed. "We do not do (think, say, feel, bother with) that sort of thing (or those kinds of people)."

Many of these opposite, lost, and despised parts of ourselves are not evil but good or neutral. Bringing them to consciousness and possibly integrating some of them into our lives is the call to individuation and spirituality of the second half of life. We begin to come to a new kind of individuality, one that is no longer measured against others or totally named by them. The more we take possession of the whole of ourselves and begin to give up competition with others as the way of affirming and validating ourselves, the more we will see the unique value of others. No longer will we exclusively identify them with their conscious or unconscious personality, their good or their evil. This is the way to a new and more godlike unconditional love of ourselves and others. It is the way to greater fullness of life.

The Struggle with Evil

Coming face to face not only with neutral qualities, but with our own, others', and the world's evil is the struggle and spirituality of the entire second half of life. Jesus never identified people with their sins. Nor, for that matter, with whom they thought themselves to be. He always saw the *more* that was there within people, and called it forth. They were healed and grew in his presence. Likewise, mature Christians seek the *more* within themselves and others and stand ready to forgive. To be forgiving is to avoid identifying others with their sins.

Part of the temptation to despair in the later years is the realization of the accumulation of a lifetime of evil. It is a consciousness of our own failures and a sickening clarity about their cost to others. While this surely has to be painfully, honestly acknowledged and grieved over, to avoid despair, we need to see the *more,* the image of God, within ourselves again and again.

Just as we love ourselves through forgiveness, so, too, we need to deal lovingly with memories of the violence, betrayals, and evil we have suffered at the hands of others. This does not mean a Pollyannaish kind of sweeping it all under the rug with a casual, "Oh well, good comes out of evil." It means facing the horror of evil. It means feeling the anger, pain, and guilt, of the reality and power of evil.

Jesus frequently confronted evil with anger. So too, the mature Christian must confront the evil that is within and without with profound anger and disgust. The mature Christian must also bear the pain, guilt, and sorrow of the world's evil and resultant suffering. But, the mature Christian does this with hope in the power of good to overcome and transcend evil, indeed, even to grow out of it. This is the paschal mystery.

Maturing Christians need to give themselves to a transpersonal cause; they need to be passionately concerned for the needs of others. Even if activity for the common good is prevented by declining physical powers, they still need to *have* a cause.

Prayerful concern and mindfulness of a cause move one into the transcendence of love, which is eternal. Jesus, in his last agony on the cross, ministered to the "good thief." In the same way, the mature Christian carries in his or her heart, even to the suffering of a deathbed, concern about both global causes (nuclear war, world hunger, ecology, AIDS, etc.) and more personal issues (addictions, handicaps, abortion, child abuse, etc.).

Each maturing person needs to discover what cause elicits compassion in him or her. Often such an affinity comes from one's own pain or the events of one's life. In any case, a maturing Christian will pursue information and take appropriate action to keep his or her care and concern alive and effective.

Living Prayer

All these loving concerns of mind and heart throughout the second half of life are prayer of a very deep kind. Such were both the prayerful living and the living prayer of Jesus who took very seriously himself, his temptations, the pain of others, and the evils of the world.

In a rhythm of action and contemplation, Jesus brought to his prayer, his explicit conscious unity with the Father, all his actions and all the events and encounters of his life. Christian maturity issues from this kind of prayerful living and living prayer. Mature Christians never hide behind prayer. They come before God in naked honesty.

Every part of us is appropriate for the intimate encounter with the One who ". . . formed my inmost being . . . knit me in my mother's womb" (Ps 139:13). No human emotion, attitude, or failing needs to be left at the door when we go to prayer. Mature prayer is the celebration and struggle of a well-worn relationship. It is surrender and screaming, loving and doubting, rejoicing and crying. It brings to God our apathy as well as our enthusiasm. It comes both with complaints about a disintegrating, aging body, waning senses, and the limitations of our mobility, as well as with our praise for the gift of length of days and growing wisdom.

In *Seasons That Laugh and Weep,*[5] Walter Burghardt, SJ, says that the key to living the later years of life well is living contemplatively. He defines contemplation as taking a long loving look at what is, and says that each word of that definition is crucial. Surely, Jesus lived this way. His preaching is filled with references to this kind of affective seeing and experiencing all that is: lilies, birds, seeds, pearls, sheep, hens, widows, coins, farmers, merchants, fishermen, children, funerals, weddings, cities, towers, barns, and sinners of all kinds. Jesus saw the kingdom of God in the midst of all of it, and all of it as revealing the kingdom of God. The "kingdom of God is like . . ." he said over and over again, finishing his sentence with the stuff of earth, each time allowing a facet of reality to speak of God's presence.

Prayer becomes the breath of the mature Christian. It fills the days, long nights, and aloneness of the elder who has suffered so many deaths.

David Steindl-Rast reminds us that gratefulness is the heart of prayer. Eucharist is thanksgiving. Life lived with such gratitude becomes a eucharist, and eucharist again and again celebrates a long life.[6]

Not taking things for granted is growth in consciousness. To be vulnerable is to move us beyond taking things for granted. The vulnerability and losses of the aging process open us to value sight and hearing and precious days and people. They open us to profound gratitude for the gifts we have and have had.

An elder who has not grown in consciousness focuses only on the many losses and diminishments of aging. The second half of life finds this person jaded, bitter, cynical, complaining, demanding, and ungrateful. The one who has grown in wisdom, age, and grace is filled with a gratitude for life and his or her own story. Even in the face of waning powers, this mature Christian is capable of receiving help from others with thankfulness rather than bitter resentment.

Gratitude always makes one feel young since, to the little child, everything is a wonderful gift. It is a profound paradox—and perhaps the greatest truth of life—that the prayerful, wise, mature Christian in the later years of his or her life can feel younger than ever before. It is even a greater paradox that those around such people know what Jesus meant when he said, ". . . unless you turn and become like children, you will not enter the kingdom of heaven" (Mt 18:2).

---

[5] See Walter Burghardt, *Seasons That Laugh and Weep* (New York: Paulist Press, 1983).

[6] See David Steindl-Rast, *Gratefulness, the Heart of Prayer* (New York: Paulist Press, 1984).

Helping Mid-Lifers in Their Spiritual Journey

Loretta Girzaitis

As I finished reading "Christian Maturation: The Later Years," my friend Louise came to mind. She is a woman in her late-fifties who had gone back to college a few years earlier and, after receiving her degree, became a court stenographer. In court, she was exposed to various life experiences, some of which shook her to her depths.

Her first experience was recording the proceedings of a young man on trial for civil disobedience. It was then that memories flooded back to the son whom she had not seen for over a decade. He left home resentful of her protectiveness and, in the interim, was jailed because of his protests at nuclear sites. Feelings of failure, doubt, longing, and worry bombarded her; she agonized over the need to forgive and be forgiven.

When she recorded family abuses, her husband's abandonment sharpened her loneliness. Her struggles to raise her children alone had been so overpowering, she had wanted to disengage herself from life. The withdrawal symptoms were painful to the point that she yearned for contact with those who might understand. Fearful that she might be misjudged and condemned, she could not take action to find companions who might listen and help her deal with her pain.

Then came the day in the courtroom when a mother's stricken and anguished face called her out of herself. This woman's son had just been convicted of murder, and Louise imagined the hopelessness and sense of failure that she felt. When court adjourned, she waited for the woman in order to express her sympathy. To her surprise, the woman embraced and thanked her for her thoughtfulness.

They headed for the court cafeteria, and when the meal was over, Louise felt that she had received greater comfort than she had given. That luncheon began a friendship that initiated a bond that deepened as both women shared stories of their lives. Without any conscious planning, they soon had other men and women coming together. During these meetings it became natural to share their life events.

Louise's story is but one example of the possibilities that await those who are open to life. Both of these women, in the second half of their lives, were living courageously, through pain, accepting it without allowing it to destroy them. Without conscious intent, they drew around themselves a core of people who, too, were looking for a common bond that would affirm and enrich their lives. Louise and her friend model for us how mid-life transitions can be handled.

In their article, Janice Brewi and Anne Brennan highlight some important themes for mid-life transition:

- We need to discern the value of life and to deepen this understanding as we mature.

- God calls us to enter creatively, cooperatively, and joyfully into the ongoing process of life.

- The second half of life is not an appendage but life's second journey, that movement by which we walk along with God in special friendship as we seek to build a world of justice and peace.

- This journeying also helps us to integrate our outer activities, which are frequently influenced by others, with our inner world, where our primary influence is the God who resides within.

- It is when we have become integrated persons that we achieve wisdom. This wisdom enhances the health and vitality of the living Body of Christ.

- It is during the second half of life that we discover the necessity and the leisure to contribute our knowledge, power, understanding, and wisdom to others and to society.

The authors also identify specific needs for people in the second half of life. It is these needs that the Church has to acknowledge if it is to serve its older adults. They include:

- understanding and becoming comfortable with one's inner life;
- recognizing the importance of ongoing conversion;
- dealing with change in self, others, society, the world;
- handling limitations and personal mortality;
- acknowledging and naming feelings for integration with self;
- sharing personal stories; and
- utilizing the benefit of experience and wisdom with others.

Those of us who work in education need to provide growth opportunities for adults in their various stages of development. Since this essay deals primarily with preparation and immersion into the second half of life, I offer recommendations dealing only with the themes and needs surfaced above.

1. Since raising a family, earning a living, establishing friendships, and surviving economic crises are particularly critical issues in the first half of life, they demand almost total attention. Because of these demands, individuals rarely find time for reflection, prayer, or planning for the future. Parishes could, therefore, provide programs for those in their late-thirties and forties and encourage them to participate in weekly sessions and weekend retreats that focus on issues of change, need for ongoing conversion, spirituality, relationships with adult children, and other similar concerns.

2. Also, at this time of life, gnawing questions surface, such as: What have I done with my life so far? Where is it leading me? What heritage am I leaving behind for others? Why have I been created? It is important that opportunities for discussing these and other questions be made available. Encouraging the formation of small groups in neighborhoods or on parish grounds where mid-lifers can gather in an accepting environment is a service that could be facilitated by a parish.

3. The formation of various groups on either a short-term or long-term basis should also be considered. Prayer groups could undertake the study of various prayer forms—scriptural, meditative, centering, contemplative—and thereby respond to different prayer needs. Support groups that deal with grief, emotions, drug addiction, and other issues might also be considered.

4. In today's society, there is an expectation that careers will change more frequently than in the past. Therefore, a parish that engages counselors to help mid-lifers discover and assess new skills, talents, and interests is providing an important service. Especially important in this area is guiding women who desire to return to college or to enter the workforce.

5. Because of the insecurity and confusion surrounding the transition from the first to the second half of life, programs dealing with mid-life need to be made available. I have been involved in leading such programs and can attest to their value. Participants confirm their benefits and praise the insights they have gained. It is clear that once individuals are enriched with these insights, they seek other means of growth in the intellectual, spiritual, and societal spheres, particularly after they are freed from previous familial responsibilities.

6. This is the time, too, when significant shifts occur in self-knowledge and the roles that friendships and community play in one's life. This is also the time when one begins to feel the need for deepening one's relationship with God. Helpful then are spiritual friends who can walk along with an individual on this journey. Yet, it is safe to say that parishes have rarely considered the need of providing spiritual directors for their constituents. This is an area that needs serious attention if the spiritual hunger of parishioners is going to be satisfied.

7. Retirement is a time of life that can be threatening and fearful. Therefore, programs that encourage productive leisure can make life meaningful. A volunteer coordinator can help retirees become "grandparents" to children without extended families, tutor non-English-speaking peoples, find service projects among the poor, and share their wisdom and expertise as consultants in various fields.

8. Also, because of the struggles that mid-lifers have experienced, they are good candidates for studying the issues of injustice. Providing them with opportunities in study clubs to examine social encyclicals and pastorals can expand their horizons and get them involved in changing systems that encourage inequalities and injustices.

9. Parish libraries need to provide books, magazines, videotapes, and other resources on mid-life and aging issues. These can then become material for discussion for both younger and older adults.

Opening ourselves to ongoing Christian maturity is a call that all of us have received from the Lord. We alone choose whether or not we will respond to it. The Church needs to provide the environment and the resources wherein each person's pilgrimage may be guided and enhanced. Otherwise, a vacuum will emerge. If the Church ignores them, then those eager for continuing growth will turn to secular sources to be nurtured. When that happens, it is likely that the spiritual element will be disregarded.

About the Authors

James J. Bacik, a priest of the Diocese of Toledo, is a theologian, writer, and campus minister.

Anne Brennan, CSJ, is the co-founder and co-director of Mid-Life Directions of Vailsberg, New Jersey.

Janice Brewi, CSJ, is the co-founder and co-director of Mid-Life Directions of Vailsberg, New Jersey.

Loretta Girzaitis is the former coordinator of adult education for the Archdiocese of St. Paul and Minneapolis.

Edmund F. Gordon is the director of religious education for the Diocese of Wilmington.

Ann Johnson is a writer and teacher, specializing in women in biblical literature.

Mary Jo Klase is the director of adult religious education for the Diocese of Fort Worth.

Jack McBride is the associate director for adult/special religious education for the Diocese of Madison.

Robert F. Morneau is the auxiliary bishop of the Diocese of Green Bay and the author of several books on spirituality.

Dennis L. O'Connor, a speaker and writer in Washington, D.C., is currently working on a book on creativity, recovery, and spirituality in personal and professional life.

Alice Stefaniak, former director of adult religious education for the Diocese of Jefferson City, is currently a doctoral student at Illif School of Theology in Denver, Colorado.